A HOMILY ON THE PASSION OF CHRIST
ATTRIBUTED TO ELISHE

EASTERN CHRISTIAN TEXTS IN TRANSLATION

A HOMILY ON THE PASSION OF CHRIST ATTRIBUTED TO ELISHE

Translated from the Classical Armenian
with Introduction and Notes

BY

ROBERT W. THOMSON

PEETERS

2000

ISBN 90-429-0841-6
D. 2000/0602/46

TABLE OF CONTENTS

ABBREVIATIONS

Aa	=	The Armenian text of Agat'angełos
CSCO	=	*Corpus Scriptorum Christianorum Orientalium*
DHGE	=	*Dictionnaire d'histoire et de géographie ecclésiastiques*
JTS	=	*Journal of Theological Studies*
MX	=	Movsēs Xorenac'i
NHBL	=	*Nor Bargirk' Haykazean Lezui*
REArm	=	*Revue des études arméniennes*
ZNTW	=	*Zeitschrift für die neutestamentliche Wissenschaft*

BIBLIOGRAPHY

Texts

Abusaid: On the Formation of Man
Yałags kazmut'ean mardoyn, ed. S.A. Vardanyan, Erevan 1974.

Agat'angełos:
History of Armenia
Agat'angełay Patmut'iwn Hayoc', ed. G. Tēr Mkrtč'ean and S. Kanayeanc', Tiflis 1909; repr. Delmar, NY, 1980. Trans.: R.W. Thomson, *Agathangelos: History of the Armenians*, Albany 1976.
The Teaching of Saint Gregory
History, § 259-715. Trans: R.W. Thomson, *The teaching of Saint Gregory: An Early Armenian Catechism* [Harvard Armenian Texts and Studies, 3], Cambridge, MA, 1970

Apocryphal Acts of the Apostles:
Armenian texts in *Ankanon Girk', III. Aṙak'elakank'*, ed. K. Č'rak'ean, Venice 1904.

Arabic Diatessaron:
A.-S. Marmadji, *Diatessaron de Tatien*, Beyrouth 1935.

Armenian Bible:
Astuacašunč' Matean hin ew nor Ktakaranac', ed. Y. Zōhrapean, Venice 1805; repr. Delmar, NY, 1984.

Basil of Caesarea:
Hexaemeron
Barsel Kesarac'i. Yałags vec'awreay ararč'ut'ean, ed. K. Muradyan, Erevan 1984.

Cyril of Jerusalem:
Catecheses
Koč'umn Ěncayut'ean, Venice 1832.

David the "Invincible" Philosopher:
Definitions of Philosophy
Sahmank' ew Tramatut'iwnk' Imastasirut'ean, ed. S.S. Arevšatyan, Erevan 1960. Trans. B. Kendall and R.W. Thomson, *Definitions and Divisions of Philosophy by David the Invincible Philosopher* [University of Pennsylvania Armenian Texts and Studies, 5], Chico, CA, 1983.

Elishe:
History of Vardan and the Armenian War
Ełišēi vasn Vardanay ew Hayoc' Paterazmin, ed. E. Ter-Minasyan, Erevan 1957. Trans: R.W. Thomson, *Elishe. History of Vardan and the Armenian War* [Harvard Armenian Texts and Studies, 5], Cambridge, MA, 1982.
Homilies
Matengrut'iwnk', First edition Venice 1838; second edition Venice 1859 [the edition used for the text translated below;

see pp. 240-354]. Partial translations in: F.C. Conybeare, "The Revelation of the Lord to Peter," *ZNTW* 23 (1924) 8-17; S. Jamourlian, "Il commento al 'Padre Nostro' di Ełišē Vardapet," *Bazmavēp* 155 (1997), 207-274; L. Leloir, "L'homélie d'Elisée sur la montagne du Thabor," *REArm* 20 (1986/87) 175-207; V. Mistrih, "Ecrits théologiques du vardapet Elisée, père de l'église arménienne," *Studia Orientalia Christiana. Collectanea* 19 (1986) 301-356; R.W. Thomson, "A Seventh Century Armenian Pilgrim on Mount Tabor," *JTS* 18 (1967) 27-33; S. Weber, "Erklärung des Vaterunsers," *Ausgewählte Schriften der armenischen Kirchenväter*, ed. S. Weber, Munich 1927, II, 273-285, "Wörte der Ermahnung über die Einsiedler," *ibid.*, 287-98; D. Welte, "Elisäus van Amathunik über die Besessenheit," *Theologische Quartalschrift* 30 (1848) 633-644.

Questions on Genesis

N. Akinean, *Ełišēi vardapeti Harc'munk' ew Patasxanik' I Girs Cnndoc'*, Vienna 1924. Trans: N. Akinean and S. Kogean, *Questions et réponses*, Vienna 1928.

Commentary on Genesis [fragmentary]

L. Xač'ikyan, *Ełišē "Araracoc' Meknut'iwnĕ,"* Erevan 1992.

Ephrem:

Commentary on the Diatessaron

L. Leloir, *Commentaire de l'Evangile concordant ou Diatessaron, traduit du syriaque et de l'arménien* (Sources chrétiennes, 121), Paris 1966. For the Armenian text see L. Leloir, *S. Ephrem, Commentaire de l'Evangile concordant, version arménienne* (CSCO 137, 145, Scriptores Armeniaci 1, 2), Louvain, 1953.

Eusebius:

Ecclesiastical History

Patmut'iwn Ekełec'oy, ed. A. Čarean, Venice 1877.

Grigor Magistros:

Letters

Grigor Magistrosi t'łt'erĕ, ed. K'. Kostaneanc', Alexandropol 1910.

Grigor Narekac'i:
Prayers
Grigor Narekac'i. Matean Ołbergut'ean, ed. P.M. Xač'atryan and A. A. Łazinyan, Erevan 1985. Trans. I. Kéchichian, *Grégoire de Narek. Le livre de prières* (Sources chrétiennes, 78), Paris 1961.

Grigor Arsharuni:
Commentary on the Lectionary
Grigorisi Aršaruneac' Meknut'iwn Ĕnt'erc'uacoc'ĕ, ed. K'. Č'rak'ean, Venice 1964. Trans. L. Froidevaux, *Grigoris Aršaruni: Commentaire du lectionnaire* (Bibliotheca Armeniaca, 1), Venice 1975.

Išox:
Book on Nature
Girk' i veray Bnut'ean, ed. S. Vardanyan, Erevan 1979.

Lewond:
History
Łewond Erēc'. Patmut'iwn, ed. K. Ezean, St. Petersburg 1887. Trans. Z. Arzoumanian, *History of Lewond*, Philadelphia, 1982.

Movses Xorenac'i:
History of Armenia
Patmut'iwn Hayoc', ed. M. Abełean and S. Yarut'iwnean, Tiflis 1913; repr. Delmar, NY, 1981. Reprinted with addditional collations by A.B. Sargsean, Erevan 1991. Trans: R.W. Thomson, *Moses Khorenats'i. History of the Armenians* (Harvard Armenian Texts and Studies, 4), Cambridge, MA, 1978; A. and J.-P. Mahé, *Histoire de l'Arménie par Moïse de Khorène*, Paris 1993.

Mxit'ar Gosh:
Lawcode
Mxit'ar Goš. *Girk' Datastani,* ed. H. T'orosyan, Erevan 1975.

Nerses Shnorhali:
Jesus Ordi
Tałač'ap'ut'iwnk' kam Bank' č'ap'aw, Venice 1928. Trans. I. Kéchichian, *Jésus Fils unique du Père* (Sources chrétiennes, 203), Paris 1973.

Physiologus:
Armenian text in N. Marr, *Sborniki Pritch Vardana*, III, St. Petersburg 1894.

T'ovma Arcruni:
History of the House of the Arcrunik'
T'ovmayi vardapeti Arcrunwoy Patmut'iwn Tann Arcruneac', ed. K'. Patkanean, St. Petersburg 1887; repr. Delmar, NY, 1991. Trans: R.W. Thomson, *Thomas Artsruni. History of the House of the Artsrunik'*, Detroit 1985.

Zohrab. See Armenian Bible.

Secondary Literature

M.R. BARNES, "One Nature, One Power: Consensus Doctrine in Pro-Nicene Polemic," *Studia Patristica* 29 (1997) 205-223.

B. COULIE, *Répertoire des bibliothèques et des catalogues de manuscrits arméniens*, Turnhout 1992.

S. DER NERSESSIAN, "An Armenian Version of the Homilies on the Harrowing of Hell," *DOP* 8 (1954), 203-224.

S. DER NERSESSIAN, "A Homily on the Raising of Lazarus and the Harrowing of Hell," *Biblical and Patristic Studies in Memory of Robert Pierce Casey*, ed. J. N. Birdsall and R. W. Thomson, Freiburg 1963, 219-34.

S. DER NERSESSIAN, *Etudes byzantines et arméniennes*, Louvain 1973, 2 vols.

S. DER NERSESSIAN, "Une apologie des images du septième siècle," *Byzantion* 17 (1944-1945) 58-87.

V. GRUMEL, *La chronologie* (Bibliothèque byzantine. Traité d'études byzantines, 1), Paris 1958).

R.H. KÉVORKIAN and A. TER-STÉPANIAN (avec le concours de B. Outtier et de G. Ter-Vardanian), *Manuscrits arméniens de la Bibliothèque nationale de France. Catalogue*, Paris 1998.

H.H. K'YOSEAN, "*Xorhrdanšanē Ełišēi meknabanakan ev čaŕagrakan erkerum*," *Ejmiacin* 1989, pt. 8, 52-60.

G.W.H. LAMPE (ed.), *A Patristic Greek Lexicon*, Oxford 1968.

S. LYONNET, *Les origines de la version arménienne et le Diatessaron* (Biblica et Orientalia, 13), Rome 1950.

L. MARIÈS, "Etudes sur quelques noms et verbes d'existence chez Eznik," *REArm* 8 (1928) 79-210.

T.F. MATHEWS and A.K. SANJIAN, *Armenian Gospel Iconography. The Tradition of the Glajor Gospel* (Dumbarton Oaks Studies, 29), Washington, D.C., 1991.

W.L. PETERSEN, "Some Remarks on the Integrity of Ephrem's Commentary on the Diatessaron," *Studia Patristica* 20 (1989) 197-202.

J.R. RUSSELL, *Zoroastrianism in Armenia* (Harvard Iranian Series, 5), Cambridge, MA, 1987.

B. SARGISEAN, *Ełišēi ew Zak'aria K'at'ołikos i T'ałumn K'ristosi Čaŕern ew Nikodimosi Awetaranē*, Venice 1910.

R.W. THOMSON, "Aspects of Armenian Biblical Exegesis: Ełišē on the Passion," *Text and Content. Studies in the Armenian New Testament,* ed. S. Ajamian and M. E. Stone (University of Pennsylvania Armenian Texts and Studies, 13), Atlanta 1994, 83-95.

R. W. THOMSON, *A Bibliography of Classical Armenian Literature to 1500 AD*, Turnhout 1995.

R.W. THOMSON, "Let Now the Astrologers Stand Up: The Armenian Christian Reaction to Astrology and Divination," *Dumbarton Oaks Papers* 46 (1992), 305-312.

R.W. THOMSON, "A Medieval Armenian View of the Physical World: the Cosmology of Vardan Arewelc'i in his Chronicle," *REArm* 23 (1992), 191-208.

R.W. THOMSON, "Number Symbolism and Patristic Exegesis in Some Early Armenian Writers," *Handes Amsorya* 90 (1976) 117-138.

R.W. THOMSON, *Studies in Armenian Literature and Christianity*, Variorum 1994.

R.W. THOMSON, *Teaching*. See s.v. Agat'angełos.

M. VAN ESBROECK, "Saint Grégoire d'Arménie et sa Didascalie," *Le Muséon* 102 (1989), 131-145.

G. WINKLER, "Our Present Knowledge of the History of Agat'angełos and its Oriental Versions," *REArm* 14 (1980) 125-41.

INTRODUCTION

Knowledge of literature written in classical Armenian has progressed in a very uneven fashion in the non-Armenian world. As in antiquity, when Greek and Latin writers only mentioned Armenia spasmodically, so in more modern times interest in Armenian writing has primarily been sparked by the light it sheds on the fortunes of other peoples and countries. Less attention has been paid to the Armenian point of view. Although the historians have received some attention, and most of the histories are now available in a translation into some western language, many other texts have been left in the obscurity of classical Armenian. As for the Armenian theological tradition, relationships with other churches have been studied more than the development of local traditions. Patristic works written in Greek or Syriac which survive only in Armenian translation have received more attention than original compositions, though the translations have usually been studied more from a linguistic point of view than with an eye to their influence on later Armenian authors. In particular, the vast mass of homiletic literature in Armenian has been almost entirely neglected.

One problem in this regard is that few Armenian texts other than the major histories have been as carefully edited. Not only does much remain unpublished, the printed texts are often unreliable; and many questions of dating and authorship remain unclear. Nor is it always obvious to what extent homilies reflect real Armenian concerns, and to what extent they are based on foreign models originally composed for quite a different milieu. An attack on the moral evils of theatres seems more appropriate for Antioch or Constantinople than for local consumption in fifth or sixth century Armenia. The use of homiletic material as evidence for social conditions is thus a tricky task. Nonetheless, as in other areas of Armenian literature, a modern translation may encourage dialogue with non-Armenian scholars, and thereby bring new insights to the study of this genre of early Armenian literature.

The following translation of Elishe's *Homily on the Passion* has two purposes. The first is to draw attention to an example of an Armenian genre little studied. The second is to stimulate discussion by those more familiar with early Christian homiletic literature than the translator, in the hope that they will be able to elucidate many of the obscurities and uncertainties. In other words, rather than wait until the text (known in many manuscripts) has been critically edited and until all Armenian problems have been solved, I regard it more useful to offer a preliminary translation as a basis for further research.

Elishe

Attributed to the Armenian author Elishe — who is famous for a classic history of the Armenian revolt against Sasanian Iran in 450[1] — are several homilies. The majority of those in the only published collection deal with biblical themes, and three with episodes from

[1] For details of the critical edition and recent translations of the *History of Vardan and the Armenian War* see the Bibliography, s.v. Elishe.

the earthly life of Christ: *On the Baptism*, *On the Transfiguration*, and *On the Passion*[2]. That on the Transfiguration has attracted some attention because of its account of monastic settlements on Mount Tabor, and some of the others have also been translated[3]. But the long *Homily on the Passion* — printed by its editor as a series of homilies on the Crucifixion, Burial, Resurrection, Appearance to the Disciples, Appearance at the Lake of Tiberias, and Preaching of the Apostles — has received less attention, save for the fact that it forms part of the material discussed by Lyonnet in his famous study of the Diatessaron and the early Armenian biblical text[4].

Nothing can be said with certainty about Elishe, the author of the *History of Vardan and the Armenian War*. This is the most famous historical work in classical Armenian after those of Movses Xorenac'i (which describes the origins of Armenia) and of Agat'angelos (which describes the conversion of Armenia to Christianity)[5]. Elishe claims to have been an eye-witness of the Armenian

[2] *Elishei vardapeti Matenagrut'iwnk'*, Venice 1838 and 1859. The second, more extended edition is that translated here. See just below for comments on the differences between the two.

[3] See the Bibliography for the articles by L. Leloir, "L'homélie d'Elisée sur la montagne du Thabor;" F. Conybeare, "The Revelation of the Lord to Peter;" R.W. Thomson, "A Seventh Century Pilgrim on Mount Tabor;" S. Weber, "Erklärung des Vaterunsers," and "Wörte der Ermahnung über die Einsiedler;" D. Welte, "Elisäus von Amathunik über die Besessenheit." The "Our Father" is studied in detail by Jamourlian. V. Mistrih, "Ecrits théologiques du vardapet Elisée," gives a translation of *On the Soul of Men*, and a general discussion of the theology of these homilies. For their symbolism see also H. H. K'eosyan, "*Xorhrdanšanē Ełišēi meknabanakan ev čaṙagrakan erkerum.*" A brief overview may be found in the article of P. Ananian, "Elisée," in the *DHGE*. A preliminary study of the *Homily on the Passion* appeared in R. W. Thomson, "Aspects of Armenian Biblical Exegesis: Ełišē on the Passion."

[4] S. Lyonnet, *Les origines de la version arménienne et le Diatessaron* (Biblica et Orientalia, 13), Rome 1950.

[5] See the bibliography for the Armenian texts and modern translations of these historians. Fuller bibliographical details on all early Armenian authors may

rebellion against Sasanian Iran, which occurred in 450-451, and its aftermath. But in some other Armenian historians such a claim is demonstrably a literary fiction[6], so it cannot be used to date Elishe. It is also likely that his work is a revised and expanded version of the shorter account of the same rebellion found in Lazar P'arpec'i, writing circa AD 500. In any event, nothing is known about the author, though a later "Life" provides legendary details[7].

In addition to the Armenian War and the homilies already mentioned, Elishe is credited with a *Commentary on Genesis*, a series of *Questions and Responses* on the same book, and a short collection of canons[8]. The common authorship of the History and the homilies is not universally accepted, though no detailed analysis of vocabulary and style has yet been made to answer the question definitively. Nor is it certain that all the homilies, the *Commentary*, and the *Questions* are by the same author. Furthermore, there exists a large number of unpublished homilies attributed to "Elishe." No proper investigation of the manuscript tradition has been made, however, nor has even the published collection of texts been fully studied as a whole[9].

be found in R.W. Thomson, *A Bibliography of Classical Armenian Literature to 1500 AD*, Turnhout 1995.

[6] Agat'angelos, for example, claims to be an eyewitness commissioned by the converted Armenian king Trdat, though the book was written more than a century later. The claim of Movsēs Xorenac'i to be a late fifth century writer is generally discounted. But this remains a controversial issue; see the arguments in the introduction to Thomson, *Moses Khorenats'i*.

[7] For the relationship between Elishe and Lazar see the introduction to Thomson, *Elishe*; the "Life" is translated on pp. 42-44.

[8] Only fragments of the *Commentary on Genesis* survive, studied in 1945 but only recently published; see L. Xac'ikyan, *Ełišēi "Araracoc' Meknut'iwnĕ."* Erevan 1992. This is a different work from the *Questions and Answers on Genesis*, published with a French translation by N. Akinean and S. Kogean, *Ełišēi vardapeti Harc'munk' ew Patasxanik' i Girs Cnndoc'*, Vienna 1924. The "Canons" are published in the 1859 edition of the *Matenagrut'iwnk'*, pp. 363-8.

[9] Mistrih's study of themes is a useful beginning.

The *Homily on the Passion*

The following translation of the *Homily on the Passion* is intended as a step on the path to solving some of these puzzles rather than as the solution itself. In the commentary to the translation I shall endeavour to identify parallels in Armenian texts, both original compositions and translations from Greek and Syriac. The *Homily* evinces no overt concern with technical theological problems, such as the Christological controversies associated with the debate over Chalcedon. Its theological language is straightforward and reminiscent of texts such as the "Teaching of Saint Gregory." But precise dating remains a problem. There is no explicit internal indication, and the texts cited for comparison are themselves often of uncertain date. The *Homily* is not quoted until the ninth century by the Catholicos Zak'aria[10]. Elishe's *History* is not cited as such until even later, in the early tenth century by T'ovma Arcruni[11]. But the late date of citation does not imply a ninth century date of composition. None of the manuscripts with extracts from these homilies precedes the twelfth century, with the possible exception of Matenadaran 1679, written in AD 981. But the second part of that manuscript was rewritten from a much later copy, and the *Catalogue* of the collection does not indicate whether Elishe's homilies come before or after the original section ends[12].

[10] See B. Sargisean, *Ełišēi ew Zak'aria K'at'ołikosi i T'ałumn K'ristosi Čaŕern ew Nikodimosi Awetaranē*, Venice 1910, where the influence of the apocryphal *Gospel of Nicodemus* on both authors is studied.

[11] For details of the Armenian text and modern translations of T'ovma see the Bibliography. T'ovma, II, 2 [p. 81 of the Armenian text] explains why Elishe's *History* does not do justice to the role of the Arcruni family; their exploits were expunged by Barsauma!

[12] For the summary catalogue of the MSS 1-10408 see O. Eganyan, A. Zeyt'unyan, P'. Ant'abyan. *C'uc'ak Jeŕagrac' Maštoc'i anvan Matenadarani*. 2 vols.,

The Armenian text used for the following translation is that of the 1859 Mechitarist edition of Elishe's works, the edition used by Lyonnet for his study of the Armenian biblical text and by the translators of other homilies attributed to Elishe. The editor of this edition gives no clue regarding the manuscript provenance of the texts.[13] On the other hand, the editor of the first (and only other) edition of 1838 indicates that he used several *čaṙĕntirk'* ["Miscellanies"] in the Venice collection and one manuscript at Paris[14]. The text of the *Homily on the Passion* as published in 1838, however, is shorter than that in the 1859 edition[15]. What is even more interesting is the fact that the manuscripts containing Elishe's homilies do not contain the whole published text as such[16]. The various sections, or even extracts from them, are found separately. This points to the popularity of the text, but

Erevan 1965, 1970. The publication of their detailed catalogue began in 1984 with vol. I of the *Mayr C'uc'ak Hayeren Jeṙagrac' Maštoc'i anvan Matenadarani*, describing MSS 1 to 300.

The oldest MSS with selections from Elishe's Homilies in the Matenadaran are no. 975, dating from 1194-5, and no. 3782, of the 12th century. The Paris MS 110 also dates from the 12th century. The earliest dated MS in Jerusalem with a text of these homilies is no. 71, written in AD 1321 [part of *On the Crucifixion*]. There are 13th century copies in Julfa, no. 422 written in 1292, and in Bzommar, no. 499 written in 1267. For details of catalogues to these and other Armenian manuscript collections see B. Coulie, *Répertoire des Bibliothèques et des Catalogues de Manuscrits arméniens,* Turnhout 1992.

[13] The manuscript tradition of the *Armenian War* has been studied by Ter-Minasian for his critical edition; but the homilies, or sections thereof, are to be found in literally hundreds of manuscripts and a proper study has not yet been made.

[14] Paris 110 written in 1194. For a full description see the Catalogue by Kévorkian and Ter-Stépanian. The extract begins on p. 300 of the printed Armenian text. The Miscellanies in Venice were the modern nos. 201, of the 12-13th century, 212 and 230, of the 13th century.

[15] It omits pp. 250-263 of the 1859 edition and ends at p. 305.

[16] This assertion is based on catalogue descriptions, not first hand examination.

suggests that the *Homily on the Passion* may have been from the very beginning a collection of shorter pieces on the different topics[17]. The general title "On the Passion" may thus be a 19th century title.

These sections all follow a common pattern. The narrative is developed as a rhetorical reflexion on the gospel text. Giving a rather free rendering of the narrative, Elishe stirs his readers to an emotional reaction, offering many figurative explanations as he proceeds. Since Lyonnet drew attention to the parallels in the biblical citations with the text of the Diatessaron, the first natural question to arise is whether Elishe — to use a convenient name, without prejudging the identity of the author — was actually following the order of the Diatessaron in his exposition of the events of the Passion. The title of the *Homily* as printed reads: "The Teaching according to the beloved John on the Passion of the Lord"[18]. The expression "Teaching" is directly reminiscent of the long section in the *History* of Agat'angelos which takes the form of a sermon preached by St. Gregory the Illuminator to the newly converted court. The over-riding theme of that "Teaching" is the fulfilment of Old Testament prophecies in the new dispensation. Prophecies also figure prominently in Elishe's Homily, but there are no exact parallels between the two texts as far as their use and interpretation of Old Testament quotations are concerned.

[17] I.e. the Sufferings [*č'arč'arank'*, the standard Armenian term for the "Passion"], pp. 240-278; the Crucifixion, pp. 278-291; the Burial, pp. 291-300; the Resurrection, pp. 300-310; the Appearance of the Lord to the Disciples, pp. 310-328; the Appearance of the Lord at the Lake of Tiberias, pp. 328-345; the Preaching of the Apostles, pp. 345-354.

[18] In the 1859 edition: *Vardapetut'iwn ěst Yovhannou sirelwoy i Č'arč'arans Tearṅ*. The 1838 edition begins further into the text, bottom of p. 241, with the title "On the Betrayal of Christ."

Numerous parallels with the work of Agat'angelos will be noted below, but Elishe did not follow the pattern of the *Teaching* for his homily. The reference in the title to John, however, raises another line of enquiry. John is the only evangelist named throughout the text; he is identified with "the disciple whom Jesus loved[19], mentioned in John 21.7 as the one who recognized the risen Lord at the Sea of Tiberias. At the start of his *Homily* Elishe remarks that we must start at the beginning with the source of life, following John who said: "In the beginning was the Word." The Diatessaron also begins with the first words of John's gospel. And since the *Commentary on the Diatessaron* by [or at least, from the circle of] Ephrem the Syrian[20] was one of the early translations into Armenian, it may be worthwhile to examine more closely the order of the Diatessaron[21] and Ephrem's *Commentary* as sources for the pattern of Elishe's exposition.

Although all Elishe's references to "the gospel" or "the evangelist" are indeed to the text of John, he does quote directly from Matthew and Luke as well (without acknowledgement). It is noticeable that Mark is not quoted alone; nor is Mark's gospel followed in those passages common to two or more of the gospels. This is in line with the general tenor of the Diatessaron and Ephrem's *Commentary*, where John is the evangelist par excellence, and Matthew is the author usually chosen to supplement his narrative. Elishe does not confine his subject matter to what is found in Ephrem's *Commentary*; nor does he include everything found in Ephrem. Nonetheless, it may be useful to list the order of events in the texts before discussing specific details.

[19] P. 332.

[20] See W.L. Petersen, "Some Remarks on the Integrity of Ephrem's Commentary on the Diatessaron," *Studia Patristica* 20 (1989) 197-202.

[21] For the text of the Diatessaron I follow the numbering of the Arabic version edited by A.-S. Marmadji, *Diatessaron de Tatien*, Beyrouth 1935.

Elishe	Ephrem	The Diatessaron
The Passion		
God the Word	I, 2	
Passover lamb	—	
Annunciation	I, 27	
Christ eats Pascha	XX, 15	
Judas and 30 pieces	—	XLIV, 7-8
Betrayal	XX, 12	
Servant's ear	XX, 13	
Christ in Gethsemane	XX, 1-11	
Arrest	XX, 12-13	
Judas repents	XX, 18	
Use of impure money	XX, 19	
Christ before Pilate	XX, 16	
Barabbas	XX, 16	
The reed	XX, 17	
Wine mixed with gall	XX, 27	
Three crosses	XX, 22	
Thieves' remarks	XX, 22-26	
"I thirst"	—	LII, 1
The women lament	—	LI, 19
Wood	XX, 21	
The Crucifixion		
Sun darkened	XXI, 4-5 [cf. XX, 28]	
Snake as type	XX, 36, 39 [cf. XX. 3]	
Death of Jesus	XXI, 1	
Tombs opened	XXI, 5	
Legs broken, blood and water	XXI, 10-11	
The Burial		
Joseph of Arimatheia	XXI, 20	

Stone at door	XXI, 21	
Christ in Hell	—	
Angels enter the tomb	—	
The Resurrection		
Mary Magdalene at tomb	XXI, 22	
Guards and high-priest	XXI, 24	
"Do not touch me"	XXI, 26-29	
Peter and John at tomb	—	LIII, 10
The clothes in the tomb	XXI, 23	
Excursus on the Trinity	—	
The Appearance of Christ		
Jesus greets disciples	—	LIV, 1
Gives the Holy Spirit	—	LIV, 15
Thomas doubts	XXI, 27	
Meaning of "twelve"	—	
Meaning of "seven"	[cf. III, 15]	
Scattering of apostles	—	LV, 5
The Appearance at Lake Tiberias		
Fishing		LIV, 25
153 fish		LIV, 35
The apostles as fishermen		
Stephen martyred		
Simon the magician		
The net and Cornelius		
Baptism		
The Preaching of the Apostles		
They go to various lands		
Simon the magician's death in Rome		
Emphasis on Peter and Rome		
Epithets for the apostles		
Sheep, goats, and cattle		

Elishe's homily (or grouping of shorter homilies) goes beyond the accounts in the gospels to cover events described in the Book of Acts. This summary of the main themes indicates that for his version of the gospels Elishe more or less confines his subject matter to what might be found in Ephrem's *Commentary on the Diatessaron* or in the Diatessaron text itself, for Ephrem did not include the whole Diatessaron in the commentary. Nor did Elishe cover all the topics found in the gospels. Only a few points, however, have been added: the discussion of the Passover lamb, Christ in Hell, the angels in the tomb, a discussion of the Trinity, and the meaning of the numbers twelve and seven. This does not mean that Elishe gives the same amount of space to the different episodes as Ephrem or that his interpretations follow those of Ephrem's *Commentary*[22].

Elishe develops his homily on the basis of a combination of the gospel accounts. He also draws on non-biblical sources in his elaborations. Much of his imagery has patristic parallels, though many of the themes are so common that his immediate sources cannot be identified. He does not mention any non-Armenian texts, save for the "History of Andrew"[23]. This is a reference to the apocryphal *Acts of Andrew*, to which Elishe had access via an Armenian translation. In addition to this text he clearly used other apocryphal documents. The *Acts of Peter and Paul* provided information not only about those apostles, but also about the legendary exploits of Simon the Magician and his spectacular death in Rome[24]. The apocryphal *Gospel of Nicodemus* lies behind Elishe's description of Christ in Hell. This was a popular theme in Arme-

[22] These points are discussed in more detail in R.W. Thomson, "Saint Ephrem and an Armenian Homily on the Passion," (forthcoming).

[23] P. 346.

[24] P. 347.

nia, and Elishe's extensive description, replete with elaborate speeches, is unlikely to have been the first Armenian account of the interval between the Burial and the Resurrection[25].

There are several general parallels with other homilies attributed to Elishe as printed in the published text[26]. But Elishe has only one explicit reference to a "previous" homily, and the passage in question does not seem to be included in the published text[27]. There is at least one close parallel with the *History of Vardan and the Armenian War*, but this does not imply that the author of the homily is identical with the author of that famous work; the wording of the death of Judas has precise verbal parallels with the description of Vasak's death in the *History*[28]. Less clear is a possible borrowing from the popular *Definitions and Divisions of Philosophy* by David the "Invincible" Philosopher. The Armenian version of this introductory text includes as an example of flux: "it is impossible to step into the same water twice"[29]. Elishe notes that one cannot drink from the same fountain twice[30]. But the theme is too common for dependence of Elishe on David to be proven. Elishe refers once to the statue at Pennada depicting Christ healing the woman with a flux of blood. This was known from the Armenian version of the *Ecclesiastical History* by Eusebius of Caesarea, and is described at some length in the early seventh century *Defence of Images* by Vrt'anes, locum-tenens of the patriarchate

[25] Elishe, p. 297-99. For the popularity of the subject see S. Der Nersessian, "An Armenian Version of the Homilies on the Harrowing of Hell," and "A Homily on the Raising of Lazarus and the Harrowing of Hell," reprinted in her *Etudes byzantines et arméniennes*, Louvain 1973, I, 437-55, 457-67.

[26] E.g., pp. 297, 344.

[27] P. 314, concerning aquatic animals on dry land.

[28] P. 261; cf. Elishe's *History*, p. 139-40.

[29] David, *Definitions and Divisions of Philosophy*, Armenian text ed. by S.S. Arevšatyan, Erevan 1960, p. 11. [See the Bibliography for the English translation.]

[30] Elishe, p. 244.

604-7[31]. Again the reference is too common for a precise source to be identified.

As noted above, only one Armenian text has extensive parallels with Elishe's *Homily on the Passion*, namely the *Teaching of Saint Gregory* in the *History* of Agat'angelos. The *History* gives the traditional account of the life of St. Gregory the Illuminator and the conversion of Armenia. An integral part of the received Armenian text is a long sermon put into Gregory's mouth, supposedly preached to the court over a period of sixty days. This is a general exposition of the Christian faith, having parallels with the *Catechetical Sermons* by Cyril of Jerusalem and the *De Fide* of Hippolytus[32]. Its emphasis is on the Old Testament as a forerunner of the New, the Incarnation of Christ, and the preaching of the gospel by the apostles. There is a good deal of common ground with the theme of Elishe's *Homily on the Passion*, although their modes of argument are quite different.

Gregory the Illuminator is not mentioned by name in this *Homily*, but a clear allusion to his vision as reported by Agat'angelos may be seen in Elishe's discussion of Christ's triple remark to Peter: "Feed my lambs; feed my sheep; feed my sheep"[33]. According to Agat'angelos, Gregory saw black goats turn into white

[31] Eusebius, *Ecclesiastical History*, VII 18. For Vrt'anes see S. Der Nersessian, "Une apologie des images du septième siècle," reprinted in her *Etudes byzantines et arméniennes*, Louvain 1973, I, 379-403.

[32] The "received Armenian text" of Agat'angelos is the Armenian in its known form. The earliest version of the work has not survived. For its complicated textual history see G. Winkler, "Our Present Knowledge of the History of Agat'angelos and its Oriental Versions," *REArm* 14 (1980) 125-41; and for the development of the *Teaching* M. Van Esbroeck, "Saint Grégoire d'Arménie et sa Didascalie," *Le Muséon* 102 (1989) 131-45. See R.W. Thomson, *The Teaching of Saint Gregory: An Armenian Catechism*, Cambridge, Mass., 1970, for an annotated translation of this long sermon.

[33] Elishe, p. 352; see Jn. 21, 15-17.

sheep as they passed through water; these gave birth to lambs, half of which crossed to the other side but turned into brown wolves[34]. The black goats are the Armenians before conversion; the white sheep, the Armenians after baptism; the brown wolves, the later apostates. Elishe borrows the distinction of black and white in his comparison of goats and sheep. But for him the goats are those who already bear the name of Christ yet work evil, not the pre-Christian Armenians. This is a rare specific allusion to a theme in Agat'angelos. More important are parallels in the technical vocabulary and the interpretation of number symbolism.

Technical Vocabulary

The first to develop a technical vocabulary for philosophical terminology in Armenian was Eznik. His treatise *On God*, which deals primarily with the problem of evil and free will, proceeds by refuting the views of the ancient philosophers, the Zurvanites of Iran, and the Christian heretic, Marcion[35]. Although his work was rarely quoted in later times, perhaps because the targets of his specific attacks no longer posed any danger to Armenian Christianity, much of the technical vocabulary that he formed became standard terminology. The later *Teaching of Saint Gregory* used these expressions in its presentation of the doctrines of the Trinity and the Incarnation. A brief presentation of the most important terms in Elishe, with parallels in Agat'angelos, may be helpful.

[34] Aa §740.

[35] For Armenian texts and modern translations see Thomson, *Bibliography*, s.v. Eznik. The technical vocabulary is the focus of L. Mariès, "Études sur quelques noms et verbes d'existence chez Eznik," *REArm* 8 (1928) 79-210.

There is a basic distinction in terms of existence between terms derived from *goy*, which render the eternal and uncreated existence of God, and the expression *linelut'iwn* for that which has been created. It is noteworthy that Elishe in the *Homily on the Passion* does not employ the stem *ē*, literally "he/she/it is," found at Ex. 3.14 for *ho on* and common in Eznik and the *Teaching*, to express divine existence[36]. He is content with two derivatives of *goy*: *miagoy*, of God as sole existent;[37] and *ink'nagoy* of God as self-existent[38]. Elishe uses several other nouns and verbs based on *goy*, but these do not necessarily refer to God or divine existence.

The abstract noun *goyut'iwn* means, for Elishe, "existence." It is used of mankind, which has a "rational existence," or of the created world, which was brought from "non-existence into "existence"[39]. The same word can also be used in the sense of "essence," as of the material essence of this world[40]. A similar expression, *goyac'ut'iwn*, only refers to created beings[41]. This is in distinction to the usage of the *Teaching*, where it is applied to divine existence[42]. The verb *goyanam* is also used of created things by Elishe: for example, "all created things come into being"[43]. And the past participle, *goyac'eal*, is applied to Christ's Incarnation in a human body[44]. The abstract noun *linelut'iwn* is only

[36] The abstract *ēut'iwn* is very common in Armenian; see Thomson, *Teaching*, p. 11.

[37] Elishe, p. 240.

[38] Pp. 279, 307, 321.

[39] P. 305 for "rational existence," *banakan goyut'iwn*; p. 337 for "non-existence," *angoyut'iwn*.

[40] P. 244.

[41] In the sing.or plural, pp. 243, 306, 321. It also carries the nuance of "essence," but again of a created being, pp. 283, 284, 289, 290, 321.

[42] *Teaching*, §391, of the "uncreated Word of God."

[43] *Amenayn linelut'iwnk' goyanan*, p. 321.

[44] P. 284.

used of created existence. It may mean created things, or the created world[45]. And it may refer to the created state, the process of being created, or even future existence[46].

The Trinity is described by Elishe as a united hypostasis, *miakan zawrut'iwn*, or *miasnakan zawrut'iwn*[47]. The word *zawrut'iwn*, whose basic meaning is "power," is applied to both the divine Trinity and to God the Word. God is a "self-existing power/hypostasis," and the same expression can define God the Word[48]. In the Teaching, however, "power/hypostasis" is not used of the Persons of the Trinity individually[49]. The Trinity is also described by Elishe as an "indivisible and unmingled hypostasis"[50].

With regard to the Incarnation, Armenian has no distinction between "body" and "flesh;" the term *marmin* is used to render both Greek terms *soma* and *sarx*. "Man" is rendered by *mard*. Elishe's vocabulary for the mode of the Incarnation is simple. His most common description is that the Son "put on" or "clothed himself" in a body [or flesh], which echoes the phrasing of the *Teaching*. "Although he was Son according to his divinity, yet through being clothed in a body he learned from the torments of death the tribulation of all living things that had fallen under the corruption of death"[51]. The Son "put on the body of our

[45] Plural at pp. 306, 309, 321 [as at n. 42 just above]; sing. at p. 240.

[46] Pp. 310, 321; 243, 323; 290 for the future.

[47] Pp. 313; 253, 308. Cf. Thomson, *Teaching*, p.13.

[48] *Ink'nagov zawrut'iwn*, p. 240, of God; p. 307, of the birth from the Virgin of God the Word. For the term "power" with regard to the Trinity see M.R. Barnes, "One Nature, One Power: Consensus Doctrine in Pro-Nicene Polemic," *Studia Patristica* 29 (1997) 205-223.

[49] Thomson, *Teaching*, p. 12.

[50] Elishe, p. 317; *anhat, anxarn zawrut'iwn*.

[51] P. 253: clothed in a body: *marmnazgec'ik*, from *marmin*, body [or flesh], and the verb *zgenum*, "I put on, clothe." For the vocabulary of the *Teaching*, see Thomson, p. 18-19.

nature"[52]. Or simply, "the Son put on humanity"[53]. Armenian has a very common verbal form in *-anam* derived from nouns. Just above we noted that the verb *goyanam* and the past participle *goyac'eal*, which derive from the stem *goy*, are applied to created things by Elishe. Likewise, in verbs derived from *marmin* and *mard*, Christ can be said to "have become flesh," *marmnac'eal*, or "become man," *mardac'eal*[54].

These expressions are common in Armenian. Much more unusual is Elishe's adaptation of a common adjective for the body, *t'anjr*, "solid" or "dense," to describe the Incarnation. The base form is used of bodies in this earthly world, and the intensive form *t'anjragoyn* of solid food[55]. The abstract noun is used of physical denseness, which is distinguished from the rational nature of mankind[56]. And the verbal form *t'anjrac'eal*, is used of the body, or of demons who take a solid form[57]. But by saying that "Christ incarnated himself into bodily form," *tanjrac'oyc' zink'n*, Elishe is creating a new expresssion for Armenian. There is, however, a parallel in Greek. *T'anjr* renders the adjective *paxys*, and the verb *paxynomai*[58] is occasionally used in the sense of "becoming corporeal."

Number Symbolism

A popular feature of Armenian theological exegesis was number symbolism. In the *Teaching* this is not so prominent as in later

[52] P. 317: *zgec'aw zmarmin bnut'ean meroy*.
[53] P.317: *zgec'aw mardkut'iwn*.
[54] Pp. 306, 275.
[55] Pp. 256; 336.
[56] Pp. 305, 323; 352.
[57] Pp. 284; 346.
[58] See Lampe, s.v. *paxyno*.

authors, but the author emphasizes the meaning of numbers such as the four points of the cross, the seven ages of the world, the twelve apostles, or the seventy-two disciples, with their biblical parallels[59]. Elishe in the *Homily on the Passion* interprets the numbers of the biblical text in three ways. The first, least important for him, is the abstract conception of mathematical properties — for example, the idea that ten constitutes numerical perfection. Such ideas are prominent in Philo, whose works gained a wide circulation in their Armenian version. Elishe prefers to point to parallels between the numbers in the New Testament and the prophetic sayings in the Old, or to parallels with features of the physical world. It may be easiest to note his interpretations by number rather than by form of interpretation.

Numbers take their origin in one; hence the cause of the world's coming into being, God, may be described as one[60]. Elishe does not speculate on the significance of the first odd and even numbers, but two is important as a constituent of seven[61]. Three is mentioned several times as a factor of larger numbers without special significance. Only once does Elishe emphasize the number of Persons in the Trinity; this is as part of his elaborate figure of the net and the 153 fishes[62]. More interesting is his attempt to resolve the dilemma in Mary Magdalene's soliloquy: Christ had foretold that he would be three days and nights in the heart of the earth, but less time seemed to have elapsed between his death on

[59] See in general R. W. Thomson, "Number symbolism and patristic exegesis in some early Armenian writers," *Handes Amsorya* 90 (1976) 117-138. Numerous texts could be added to the evidence collected there, especially the commentary on the Lectionary by Grigoris Arsharuni, translated by L.M. Froidevaux, *Grigoris Aršaruni: Commentaire du Lectionnaire*, Venice 1975.

[60] Elishe, p. 321.

[61] P. 321.

[62] P. 335; for the net see below.

the cross and her coming to the tomb after the sabbath. Elishe does not resolve this apparent discrepancy[63].

Four is an altogether more significant number. Elishe stresses that the Cross has four angles or points. This had been a major theme in the *Teaching*, where the four points refer not only to the four corners of the world, but also indicate those above in heaven and those in hell[64]. Elishe does not think of the Cross as pointing upwards, thus indicating God the Father. But he does regard it as indicating the inclusive nature of the Redemption[65]. The whole world also reminds him of the four elements, though he does not expand on the contrast of the hot and cold, dry and wet, or their various combinations[66]. The net which Elishe presents as an elaborate image of the preaching of the apostles also has four sides.

No biblical parallel for the number five is adduced. It is mentioned as a component of the more important number seven; and Elishe refers to the five planets[67]. For the number six Elishe stresses that the six days of God's creative activity are parallel to the six ages of this corrupted world. This is a more significant theme in the *Teaching*, where the theme of the age to come is elaborated[68]. Elishe has only one reference to the seventh age, which he equates with the sabbath[69]. Other associations of the

63 P. 301. Afrahat, XII 7, tackled the problem. He resolved it by starting the period of three days and nights on the evening of the Last Supper.

64 Elishe, p. 271; cf. *Teaching*, §488-90.

65 P. 278.

66 Pp. 278, 321. For references to Armenian authors who discuss such matters see R.W. Thomson, "A medieval Armenian view of the physical world: the cosmology of Vardan Arewelc'i in his Chronicle," *REArm* 23 (1992) 191-208.

67 Pp. 280, 321.

68 Elishe, pp. 254, 315, 321, 324; cf. *Teaching*, §667-71. Elishe, p. 315, also notes that the term "Lord" appears in Genesis for the first time only with regard to the sixth day.

69 P. 324.

number seven are suggested frequently. In the cosmos there are seven spheres, which Elishe describes as levels of air separated by an open interval. He does not make it clear whether or not these are the carriers of the seven moving orbs, the sun and moon plus the five planets[70]. Twice Elishe refers to the seven senses, though not to sight, hearing, taste, touch, and smell, as one might expect. He reaches the number seven by counting two eyes, two ears, taste, understanding and desire; or by adding two eyes, two nostrils, and two ears to the mouth[71]. From the biblical narrative he stresses that there were seven disciples to whom Jesus revealed himself at the lake of Tiberias, and refers to the seven gifts of the Spirit without describing them individually[72].

Eight comes up only in connection with the eight day interval between the appearances of Jesus to the disciples, when Thomas remained in doubt. These eight days have a parallel in the eight days before circumcision[73]. Like other Armenian authors Elishe regards the number ten as numerical perfection, though he offers no arguments to demonstrate the point. Ten is particularly significant as a mystery for Christ's passion, for it recalls the tenth day of the month when the lamb was chosen for the pascha, as in Ex. 12.3[74].

Elishe adduces more biblical parallels for twelve than for other numbers. Most importantly, there are twelve apostles. Parallels include the sons of Jacob and the twelve tribes; the stones of Joshua; the twelve baskets; the twelve years of the woman with a

[70] P. 321, his longest description of the physical cosmos. There are also seven fixed stars.

[71] Pp. 280; 321.

[72] Pp. 329; 323.

[73] P. 315.

[74] P. 244. See also below for the three tens in thirty.

flux of blood[75]. There are twelve regions of the world where the apostles preached, and these twelve apostles figure as holders of the net which contained the 153 fishes. Then there are twelve stars, whence the astrologers deceived and deluded men. This seems to be a combination of the five planets and the seven fixed stars, omitting the sun and moon[76]. There are twelve hours in the night and twelve in the daytime. Since the world had fallen into corruption, Elishe notes twelve aspects of these afflictions: abandoning God; the worship of man-made objects; sacrifice to insensible objects; indifference to corruption; killing one's fellow-image; avarice; hatred; theft; rapine; falsehood; pride; death[77].

The thirty pieces of silver offered to Judas are interpreted as three tens. Each ten, says Elishe, refers to a fault imputed to the Jews. They dishonoured the ten commandments; they denied the salvation of Moses; they disbelieved in the ten gifts of the earth. What these last might be is not explained[78]. Fifty, which has a parallel in the Old Testament jubilee, is a constituent of the number 153. These fish caught in the lake of Tiberias by Peter and his companions give Elishe an opportunity to expound the meaning of the net, his most elaborate simile in this *Homily on the Passion*. The apostles are the fishermen, and the net contains bait, which is Christ. The metaphor of bait or hook for Christ is common in Armenian[79], but the following elaboration of the theme is not found in other early Armenian writers. There are two lines to the

[75] Pp. 325-28.

[76] P.327; cf. p.321.

[77] P. 325. I have found no parallel to this list.

[78] P. 250. The significance of the three is not explained. Elishe elsewhere divides numbers into their factors without further comment. Thus on p. 321 twelve is described as 3 times 4 or 2 times 6.

[79] See, for example, Aa, §81; Lewond, p. 83; Grigor Narekac'i, *Prayer* 93; Grigor Magistros, *Letter* 67; Nerses Shnorhali, *Jesus Ordi*, line 1119.

net, and four ends to the lines; these are grasped by the twelve apostles in threes. There are four sides to the net, which embraces the whole world. All the factors of twelve are thus introduced, since six is but twice three[80].

Observations

The history of Armenian homilies is yet to be written. But this brief review of the main points in the *Homily on the Passion* attributed to Elishe, indicates many features that it has in common with other early Armenian compositions. Its author is primarily anxious to impart a sympathetic attention to the biblical narrative. The homily is more contemplative in tone than exhortative, and not overtly concerned with inculcating moral virtues. In keeping with this more emotional approach, the language is somewhat repetitive and verbose, not tightly argued like the treatise by Eznik *on God*. Elishe is not greatly involved in matters of Christological import or the controversies over matters of ritual, which eventually split the Armenian church from other churches of the East. The technical vocabulary employed is reminiscent of Agat'angelos and the Teaching of Saint Gregory, but not entirely consistent with that basic text. So although precise indications of its date are lacking, the homily would seem to belong to the period before Armenian theological terminology became fixed.

Like most early Armenian theologians Elishe was much interested in number symbolism. And his insistence on Old Testament parallels for the interpretation of Christ's activity in this world is shared by all Armenian writers. He does not quote his sources,

[80] Pp. 335-38.

save for apocryphal texts and the canonical biblical books; but in that too he is typical of Armenian authors. The influence of this homily on later Armenian literature is difficult to judge, inasmuch as the homily itself is little known and texts of a similar genre where its ideas might be reflected remain mostly unstudied and unpublished. The purpose of the following translation is precisely to open this field of enquiry, and to encourage a wider circle beyond the small number of scholars of classical Armenian to look at an unfamiliar eastern Christian text.

ELISHE

The Teaching according to the beloved John on the Passion of the Lord

[p. 240] I am very greatly amazed at our audacity, to what heights it has attempted to reach. Not because it reached them was there surprise, but rather that it desired to attain them and did not succeed — just as our impiety plans to be carried to the extreme height, yet crawls along the ground working all [sorts of] wickedness. For many are the offspring of the wicked part, and worthless are the fruits which are savoured as counsels therefrom. Base deeds, impure delights and dissolute desires, loves of obscenities and longings for the insatiable, preoccupation with wealth and ease in the world — these are quite unable to look upwards and see the spiritual riches in their souls and bodies. If you approach them a little and come up against those riches, you will laugh at this lower sun. You will henceforth keep away from vicious habits, and as long as you are in the body you will raise yourself up above all these visible things. Just as the great evangelist John begins—not from the sea, not from dry land, not from just men, nor from the place whence appeared the source of life, not even from heaven or earth of this created universe. Whence then must one start? From the one without beginning — through hours and times, ages and eternity, to reach the incomprehensible and ungraspable, the sole existent[1] hypostasis whence derives all the wonderful creation.

"In the beginning was the Word, and the Word was with God, and the Word was God,"[2] he who is the cause of everything. [p. 241] So hearing this truth, do not remain a transgressor in this life and temporal world. But with that same apostle, let us fly to the incorporeal realm, seeing there God the Word incarnate. And let us pray the all-merciful Lord to pour out the light of his grace into our souls and bodies, and that the eyes of our minds may be illumined, as we have a narrator of his holy passion and illuminating resurrection who befits his glory. By him the church is greatly glorified and has many spiritual fathers, apostles, prophets, true shepherds, who gained heavenly treasure. But how many are the spiritual fathers, and how many virtuous sons they have! And how many are the great inheritances, and even more the newcomers and heirs! If the first [fathers] in their own generations were found [to be] perfect in labours, alert in vigils, firm in faith, and looking from afar with great asceticism there beside themselves saw the Lord of all, who came for the salvation of all, they were not deprived of his life-giving gospel. They accepted and believed, and remain firm until today. So now the sons must run the same course as their fathers, holding the same faith, taking upon themselves the same labours, being long-suffering with the same patience, and must watch for his second coming and observe his gospel. When we reflect on and are instructed in all this, broken in and made familiar with the labours of our spiritual fathers, and we appear as those fathers' spiritual sons — then through the help of the

[1] Sole existent hypostasis: *miagoy zawrut'iwn*; see the Introduction.

[2] Jn. 1.1, also the first biblical citation of the Diatessaron after the Preface.

Spirit we shall be able to gain the inheritance of the holy fathers which they handed down to us. For behold, the first ones sowed and nourished, those in the middle harvested and laboured, and we have come and entered into the labours of the first.

So let us, the last ones, not be slow and lazy, lest perchance we be found deprived of the beginning and increase, and failing to attain the goal like wicked heirs, we make ourselves die of hunger. Behold we all know that the church has great riches and heavenly treasure, which no one can comprehend or reckon in numbers. **[p. 242]** But I shall summarise the apogee of the heavenly fruits, describing [only] part of many, so that by one part all the parts may become apparent. For although you may all be absolutely full of divine riches, I, by no means advanced in deep knowledge, will not bring you to new faith by abbreviating or relating new and strange words. Heaven forbid that such things should be said or heard in the holy church! But for compassion of the love of the Lord of all, and for affection for our first fathers who by their faith became firm pillars and victors of the church[3], we wish according to our little knowledge to apply ourselves to work day and night, to be unceasing in reading the heavenly testaments and in attending to the visible mysteries, so that the radiance of the holy Spirit may shine upon us, and that through the infallible paths which lead along the narrow way we may surely enter the narrow gate to the great heavenly capital.

So[4] behold we have reached the mid-point, which is the last beginning and the first end. "Let this month, says [scripture], be for you the beginning of the months in the months of the year"[5].

[3] Pillars of the church: Gal. 2.9.

[4] The 1836 edition [henceforth A] begins the homily "On the Betrayal of Christ" here, [p. 234].

[5] Ex. 12.2.

Truly the new splendid power of the holy Spirit legislates through Moses, who grasps the month, and by means of the month leads and brings [the argument] to the creation. "This first month, he says, will be for you the beginning of months," which is the month Areg[6]; because at the beginning of creation this month does not exist, but [only] a day and beginning, and a day again new-born and month pre-eminent, and time of spring. For at the dispersing of the waters from the face of the earth and with the appearance of the dry land a voice was sent down from above: "Let the earth bring forth plants of sown pasture and of fruit-bearing trees"[7]. Then the earth heard the heavenly command like an intelligent and rational [creature], and setting to work brought forth its produce. According to each one's kind appeared together the finished product of pasture and trees. Not only individual [trees] according to kind and likeness, but also each kind of fruit, mature **[p. 243]** and brought to perfection. This [was] the same month in the days of the catastrophe of the flood, when for the whole year the just man was held and enclosed inside the ark. But when mercy descending from above commanded him to come out of the ark, and all who were with him, this month became the beginning of months in the days of the year. And once more the earth became verdant and nourished all the living things on it, so that creatures might increase and multiply in accordance with their original existence.

[6] Areg is the eighth month of the Armenian year. But the year was mobile; only from the 12th century [see Grumel, p. 143—in the time of the Catholicos Gregory III, 1113-1166], when Navasard was fixed as 11 August, did Areg necessarily fall in spring. Nonetheless, it renders Nisan in the Armenian of Esther, 8.9; and in the Armenian version of Cyril of Jerusalem, *Catecheses*, p. 280, "the month Areg" is equated with spring. Ephrem's *Commentary* does not mention Areg here.

[7] Gen 1.11ff. But the text is not that of Zohrab or of the Armenian text of Basil's *Hexaemeron*, V.

Thus Moses, who became worthy of the holy Spirit to describe the coming into being of creatures, places this month at the beginning as the begining of the world's creation and of the disaster of the waters which destroyed the world. He shows this month as the beginning of the appropriate numbers of years. Moses, after saving the people from Egyptian servitude, legislated for the Hebrews this great festival, saying: "Let this month be for you the beginning of the months in the months of the year." Not only saving them from cruel servitude, but also freeing them from heathen festivals, he ordered them on the fourteenth of the month[8] to sacrifice a lamb, and to celebrate the feast in each one's house at night — in which also would be fulfilled the illuminating mystery of the resurrection of Christ.

Henceforth this month is found as the beginning of creation, the basis of the establishment of the growth of existent beings, and of the number of hours and times and centuries to the end of the world. The sacrifice of reconciliation was offered in it, just as we said above in the days of the just one; and [it was] the reason for freedom from oppressive servitude for the seed of Abraham. So henceforth we are redeemed from this earthly servitude into freedom. In this space, brethren, let us labour attentively; like virtuous husbandmen let us plough deeply and with great effort soften the harshness of this earth, so that digging deeply we may pull out the harmful dog-grass[9] deeply rooted around the word; that the grains of corn, beautifully sown, may make the owner of the field happy. For if anyone despise the iota point, which is one of the smallest letters yet occupies the [same] setting as the greatest, he will be found to be lacking in his art. **[p. 244]** How much

[8] Ex. 12.6.

[9] Dog-grass: *sēz*, as Basil, *Hexaemeron*, Arm. text p. 128; the Greek *agrostis*.

more should we fear to pass over the great gifts of the holy Spirit, of whose heavenly riches the beginning and middle and end are filled![10] If I begin from a single one and go on to the hundreth and reach the thousands and dare to attain many myriads, there still remain far more than these.

Nevertheless, take for yourself a perfect simile, whereby your mind may come to a true conviction. When in thirst you make for the fountain, you and the many more with you will not be able by your drinking to dry up the flowing of the fountain, nor will you drink the same water as you drank before. And if you sit at the fountain you will not meet with the same water a second time[11]; nor again will you see anything foreign mingled in it; nor will yesterday's appear to you again today. So if the nature of water, undivided in its course, shows such great wisdom to man, how much more will the divine words, if you give them as drink to thirsty souls! Never will you be filled with heaviness, but lightened you will desire the same. Although their taste and nature are the same, yet types of wisdom have different savours in the minds of philosophers; and all, summed up in the one, look to the truth.

But what is this, that he orders to take hold of the lamb on the tenth day of the month[12], the living creature in the midst of living ones, the voiced one in the midst of rational ones? Behold the mystery is clear; if anyone wishes, he is able to see it. The decad contains numerical perfection, and number [contains] the material essence[13] of this world. For by means of the material the teaching of perfect instruction will grasp bodily things. And at the full

[10] Elishe likes triads; cf. pp. 241, 351.

[11] Cf. David, *Definitions*, p. 11, but of a river, not a fountain.

[12] Ex. 12.3.

[13] Material essence: *niut'akan goyut'iwn*.

moon[14] in the evening time the sacrifice is offered; which clearly shows the blemish of the incompleteness of the ordained feast. But because it is a great mystery of the true lamb of God[15], who is to come and save Israel, not merely from Egypt, but from servitude to Satan, the blood of the lambs over each one's lintel is indicated; and it saves everyone's **[p. 245]** house from the scourges by which the Egyptians were struck, from the greatest to the least. Just as cultivators rejoice in the sight of the blossom of trees before the ripening of the fruit, so also will we rejoice in the mystery of this feast until the lamb of God is sacrificed, which is the feast of salvation for Jews and Gentiles. Since the Israelites did not have their own land to inhabit and a temple in God's name for all to gather in, nor did they [yet have] the tribe of Levi ordained to the priesthood, the grace of God was considered sufficient to make each individual a temple and habitation of God, and for there to be priests in every house.

Nonetheless, let us diligently press on to the perfect command of Moses, which in actuality ordains the lamb of God for the sons of Israel but potentially from afar makes allusion to the sons of God[16]. "Do not eat it raw,"[17] he says, which is carrion of an animal. "Nor cooked with water," which is excess and licentiousness in this world. And not at all, "Do not eat," which is the deceit of denial[18]. "But eat it roasted," which is an unadorned consummation of heavenly fire. "Eat quickly," not lingering as if to eat partially of the body, but by the power as of fire with all parts of its

[14] I.e., the fourteenth day, see Ex. 12.6; *lusalir* does not appear in the biblical text.

[15] See further below, p. 290, for the Lamb and Christ.

[16] In actuality... potentially: *gorcov... zawrut'eamb.*

[17] Ex. 12.9.

[18] Denial: or "apostasy."

being. "The head, with the feet and entrails," he says. And very appropriately he bids to eat the first created head and supporting feet of the body with the nourishing entrails, passing over the passion, that you may valiantly be saved by the three. "But what remains over from the three until the morning,"[19] he commands to burn, which is sin and lawlessness. Again, by saying "girdles round your waist, and shoes on your feet, a rod in your hand, torches lighted,"[20] all these are signs of the firmness of courage; right now the haste of the people[21] in leaving, but in the future to be a colony in this very world of life. Because girdles indicate valiant war, and rods the royal and disciplinary functions; but shoes fearlessness of the road, harmlessly stepping on poisonous snakes; [**p. 246**] and lit torches the unquenchable illumination of the mind of men, which sees the Lord of the mystery from afar as nearby, most clearly in saying: "Do not break its bone, and do not leave it until morning"[22]. As indeed happened, which we shall see in the present discourse.

So if Moses previously trained the people to such a clear mystery, in which the secrets were later to be revealed by God, and the prophets preached the same through the same Spirit, and the just believed, and all the people waited for the coming of the Lord— as the Samaritan woman said: "When the Messiah will come, he will tell us everything"[23] — then this same Lord who fulfilled this expectation for the people, in the same month of Areg was announced by the angel to the holy virgin in Nazareth[24], in order

[19] Ex. 12.10; Elishe adds "from the three."

[20] Torches lighted: not in Ex. 12.11.

[21] People: *gałut'*, lit. "colony."

[22] Ex. 12.10. "Do not break its bone," is found in the LXX and Armenian, not the Syriac or Hebrew.

[23] Jn. 4.25.

[24] Areg: as in Ephrem, *Commentary*, I 27.

that he might make this same month the beginning of this new salvation. And the lamb of God entered and was enclosed in the virgin's womb, being there nine months, in order that he might open the eyes of the blind by reminding them of the slaughter of the lamb which took place in Egypt, so that those who grew and attained the measure of perfect knowledge might perchance not be deprived of the lamb of God, who was to save them from the ancient indissoluble bonds of sin. Just as the lamb of God himself summed up all delay in the thirty year period[25] and still more by his years among the sons of the people, by his birth and revelation at baptism[26]; just as he completed all the working of signs in Judaea and decided on the election of the apostles from these same sons, and with continual instruction taught them all from the law and the prophets, that: "They all preached about my coming," saying to the Apostles: "I am not sent anywhere, save only to the lost sheep of the house of Israel;"[27] similarly he confirmed the gospel of the fathers by submitting to circumcision, undertaking to make acquaintances and friends among all. He opened the gate for taxmen and sinners to approach him. He drove out demons from the borders of the chosen race. **[p. 247]** He healed pains and torments. They who with faith approached him were shaken out of themselves. Similarly, and what is greatest of all, in many places and on many occasions he bound death and placed it beneath his own victorious power. He reclaimed the dead alive from the impious tyrant. He wiped every tear from all eyes; mourning and sadness fled from before him; hatred was persecuted and avarice opposed; darkness fled and light reigned.

[25] Lk.3.23.

[26] Christ's birth, revelation [epiphany], and baptism form one festival in the Armenian tradition.

[27] Mt. 15.24.

When they had so ordered and arranged all this, the priests and high-priests, struck by the pangs of envy, covered their eyes from the light of the truth. Blocking their ears, they did not wish to heed the law and the prophets or to receive the preaching which fulfilled the announcements of the prophets. But despite all these benefits, they turned in opposition and prevented the people from heeding the life-bestowing teaching. Then he came to the same month, which from the beginning indicated the mystery of the Life-giver[28]; and the Lord of all, for love of the sons of God, feeling the same mercy wished to celebrate the same Pascha with them in joy, that perchance the darkness of envy might be dispelled from their thoughts, and the eyes of their minds might be opened, which they had willingly blinded, and they might recognise the Lord of the feast who had come to give life to all creatures who were dead in their sins.

But now hear the enormous wickedness. "When the feast of unleavened bread which they call Pascha had drawn near, says [scripture],"[29] they knew that Jesus was coming to the multitude of the people to teach them. They were struck with fear and were greatly frightened lest perhaps he either open [the eyes of] the blind, or heal the paralysed, or cleanse those possessed by demons. Especially if he were to raise someone who had died, all the people would believe in him. Because of this fear the high-priests and scribes[30] took counsel and told the princes and instructed the multitude of the people, that where anyone might see him he should indicate him, **[p. 248]** so that they themselves,

[28] Ephrem, *Commentary*, XX 15, notes that Christ ate the Pascha in the month of Areg.

[29] Lk. 22.1.

[30] Scribes: *meknič'k'*, lit. "Interpreters," not biblical. See also pp. 296, 323, where it is used of Pharisees, and p. 339 where it is used of Sadducees.

armed as with weapons, might kill him wherever they might find him.

After they had failed by these methods, a helper was found for them who from the beginning had been dwelling in their hearts, by means of a certain mediator who by name was among the apostles and became an accomplice to the evil-minded priests, just as the gospel clearly indicates: "Satan, it says, threw into the heart of Judas to betray him to them"[31]. Do you see that they were accomplices — not to the high-priesthood, but to the devilish deed? He went to them and said: "What will you give me, and I shall betray the teacher?"[32] and they offered him immediately the sum of thirty [pieces of] silver. O mad ones, and not priests; because although he was wickedly betraying, yet he declared a good name: "teacher," he said, and not thief or murderer or anyone else from among the evil-doers of this world. Because you promise your silver, why do you not question his works? "For what evil deeds do you betray him into our hands?" But perhaps you were afraid to ask: "For what evils did you betray him?" You did well in this, because you yourselves know and have comprehended that: "Deceit was not found in his mouth, nor lawlessness in his deeds,"[33] whereby no man can reproach him.

Well then, I ask you, why did you give your silver, and whence do you give it, and why thirty pounds?[34] If he was guilty of death, as you say, do not lose your silver. No man buys a condemned man for silver and puts him to death. Let him go; his sins accuse him. Take note of his works, because his wicked deeds hand him over to death. I know that you are true, and especially wise and

[31] Jn. 13.2.
[32] Mt. 26.15.
[33] Is. 53.9; cf. 1 Pet. 2.22.
[34] Pounds: *litra*. Cf. above, where *kšir*, "sum, measure" was used.

high-priests and greater in knowledge than all — you know. Behold an informer from among his disciples, ask and write down the works of his teacher. Begin from where he began his activity[35], there at your feast you will find many Galileans. You will find at the marriage the water turned into wine; and at Capernaum the 5,000 sated from five loaves **[p. 249]** and twelve baskets full remaining[36]. And if you ask at Nain you will see the widow's only son raised from the dead[37]. If you enter the house of the high-priest you will see the same one. And if you enter the land of the Gergesenes, not only will you see the young man cured who had been possessed of many demons, but also the demons drowned in the lake[38]. If you enter the city of Pennada, not only will you see the woman healed, but also the Lord's statue standing [there] and the cured one grasping hold of the Lord's hem, and under the same statue a root growing which offers healing to the afflicted[39]. But I know that you are not able to go afar off, because you do not so wish. Enter Bethany; near there ask Lazarus where he went or whence he came[40]. And if you do not wish to ask him, because he relates evil about you concerning the future place which is prepared for you, then ask the blind man of Jericho whom he healed from afar by his voice[41]. If you reckon these to be pretexts, there

[35] I.e. Jn. 2.11, "This beginning of miracles did Jesus in Cana of Galilee;" cf. also Mt. 4.17, "Jesus *began* to preach [in Galilee]."

[36] Mt. 14.15-21, Mk. 6.41-44, Lk. 9.13-17, Jn. 6.9-13. But this miracle did not take place at Capernaum, which Jn. 6.17 defines as "over the sea" from the site of the miracle.

[37] Lk. 7.11-15.

[38] Mt. 8.28-33.

[39] Mt. 9.20. For the statue of Jesus see Eusebius, VII 18, quoted in Vrt'anes, "Apologie des images;" see Der Nersessian, I, p. 383. Cf. also Mathews/Sanjian, p. 120.

[40] Jn. 11.1.

[41] Jn. 10.46-52.

in that same city regard in Bethesda the thirty-eight years[42]. The bed will shout forth your mercilessness. And asking in Siloam[43], you will see the man blind from birth to have received sight. He is well informed to give answer.

So for what act is the teacher betrayed into your hands? If you know and the deeds are evil, then hear them now; write them down and show them to your judge, so that he may be betrayed by his own deeds. But if his deeds are good, as indeed they are good, you are not only put to shame at being worsted, but all your colleagues with you. And he who betrayed him is not only worthy of opprobrium, but also of many torments for having denied such grace. If you are lovers of the truth, you yourselves will exact vengeance from him, because he who looks at him would not repay evil with good. But because you did not do this—but you even give money to him, and not from your own resources but from the holy gifts of the temple—are you not indeed reproved and reprimanded? For it is not man's treasure but God's all-holy temple that you are breaking up and robbing. Not for the ransom of prisoners, nor for gifts to the poor, [**p. 250**] but for the price of just blood — not any man's, but that of the Son of God.

So then rightly the prophet Zechariah foreknew your wickedness, you who offer much reward to your crooked false prophets because they expressed the will of your evil persons and were even more praisers of the evil of your ways. The true prophet said: "If it seems good to you that such [persons] should have limitless wages, give me too my price. But if not, make account so that I too may know"[44]. And they immediately weighed and gave into

[42] Jn. 5.5. But Bethesda was at Jerusalem, not Jericho.

[43] Jn. 9.7.

[44] Zech. 11.12; but divergent from Zohrab.

his hands thirty [pieces of] silver. This was in the eyes of the prophet unbearable bitterness, to see in that the great and terrible evils which the people were to do. He was unable to mitigate the seriousness of the events; so he took and cast it into the furnace of the house of the Lord, that perchance they might be shamed out of their mad deeds, which even surpassed the impiety of the demons. But they do not increase nor do they subtract from their complete evils. They keep the number thirty, and bring and offer it to the betrayer so that they might buy the divine blood. Not by chance nor suddenly deciding on it, but by an old plan[45] which they fulfilled against the Renewer of all in their wickedness.

Now if you were to change the number thirty of your silver into gold, it would be divided into three fifties; and if into the same amount of silver, it would consist in three tens. By the first ten they dishonoured the ten commandments; by the second ten they denied the salvation of Moses; by the third ten they disbelieved in the gifts of the earth. Furthermore, through the same triple number they changed the Father for the calf in the desert; and stoning the prophets they embittered the holy Spirit; and by the remainder of this same number they bought the holy blood for themselves and their sons for ever.

Because they were enraged to angry envy like beasts of the desert, they paid no attention to the honourable feast[46]. The priests and high-priests, elders and Pharisees, and he who was leader **[p. 251]** of the temple gathered together with all the multitude, armed as with weapons. And they had this further guide to whom they gave the silver from the temple, and with him their assistant the incorporeal and immaterial Satan, and the time of

[45] Plan: *xorhurd* also means "mystery."

[46] A, p. 242, "On the Betrayal of Christ" ends here.

evening [as a] help, that in the time of darkness they might fall into the pit of destruction. "Whom I kiss, he says, is the one; seize him and lead him away carefully"[47]. For the ill-omened greeting he receives the appropriate retribution. "To whom I shall dip in the dish and give, he says, he it is who will betray me"[48]. The "I shall dip" means I shall wash away blessings. Whose heart has become the dwelling place of the treacherous enemy, there the divine grace does not linger. But where the divine grace does not dwell, he is trampled by the passers on the road.

But Peter who was full of benevolent zeal, especially when he saw his fellow-disciple with them, was unable to endure the satanic power; because he had heard from the omniscient Lord: "He who has a sword, let him take it; and who has not, let him buy one and bring it"[49]. What is the command of such a statement as this? For it is obvious to the wise that he likened the truth to a sword. Whoever has piety let him stand firm. And whoever is a little weak, let him buy — not a sword from some man, but the truth from the Son of Man; not for the price of silver, but with his own blood. For the sword has come to strike not only the visible proximity but also each one in soul and body. This is the natural and the acquired sword. Now Peter had both: the natural, in the love for the master which he had through the holy Spirit; the acquired, whereby he cut off the servant's ear[50]. Very fittingly the servant's and not a free man's, that of sin and not of virtue; the refractory ear, not the head — the honoured

[47] Mt. 26.58, and parallels.

[48] Jn. 13.26.

[49] Lk. 22.36. Cf. Ephrem, *Commentary*, XX 13; but Elishe does not follow Ephrem's exposition.

[50] Mt. 26.51, Mk. 14.47, Lk. 22.50, Jn. 18.10. Acquired, natural: See Lampe, s.v. *epitketos* for the contrast with *phusikos*.

part — and not all of it. For there is nothing so similar to servitude as the sensation of the mind. Because the eye is affected by a [physical] encounter, but the mind by the spiritual; and the ears have been prepared for listening, the eyes for seeing; and intelligence thence [**p. 252**] produced the response. The olfactory sense of the nose aroused the taste-buds to the choice of distinguishing. And through these senses all tangible things receive careful observation.

It is something very difficult for the ears to preserve silence, as this is oppressed by unworthy sounds. Not only does it remain a servant, but it is doubly enslaved to captive sensations. So by striking off the servant's ear he indicated the non-observance and disobedience of man from the very beginning. But because there are many reasons why the benevolent Lord of heaven and earth came to heal all our infirmities and to fill and to complete the imperfections of our minds, his benevolence did not pass over the servant's ear. But picking it up right there, he replaced it[51], showing the spot to be unwounded and unscarred — which is a sign of the return of the sinner to penitence. And he speaks to all with pleasing words and a sweet voice.

But because his power was invincible, although he spoke very humbly, nonetheless by saying "I, I,"[52] God incarnate twice presented to them his nature; but they did not understand. Consequently, having pity on those who despised even their benefactor, three times at the same place he fulfilled the word. He orders Peter to put back his sword[53]; and he hands himself over on behalf of his disciples to those who arrested him; and at the same time he also fulfils the command of the Father by drinking the cup of

[51] Lk. 22.51.
[52] Jn. 18.8?
[53] Jn. 18.11.

death. Because he was unlying God[54], he became truthful man; and fearless through his indubitable divinity, he was handed over to those who arrested him. But in his human nature with fearful and beseeching prayers he begged from Him who could save him from death, not something insignificant or presumptuous, seen in a confused dream; but as a provident and prudent shepherd of living and rational sheep he foresaw what would happen.

Then[55] taking the disciples he came to the place which the prophets had previously indicated: **[p. 253]** "I shall gather, says [scripture], all the races of the earth, and shall bring them down to the valley of Josaphat. And there I shall set them to judge all the races round about"[56]. Not because the prophecy had previously declared were the events fulfilled involuntarily; but the same God the Spirit himself spoke through the prophets whatever would occur — not today, whatever transformation occurred from the beginning in accordance with the will of the first man in his freedom. And because the events were not necessary but in accordance with the advice of the enemy and the inclination of the evil spirit, they neglected the inclinations to become more fruitful than the most worthless fruit. Because the Lord of all had not come for condemnation, but to save from servitude and renew into freedom, he asked in prayer from Him who had sent him to deliver the world from error and bring it to the Father's kingdom.

So he saw that in this place all creation had arrived to witness the death of the Son of God. He left the disciples in the lower place, and he himself went up a little to a higher place. He fell on

54 Unlying: *ansut*, Titus, 1.2.

55 This is out of sequence according to the gospels and Ephrem's *Commentary*.

56 Joel 3.2.

his face, bent down and kissed the surface of the ground, poured holy tears on the holy piece of earth, and removed the first curse[57]. Then he stood up, and looking upwards said to the Father in prayer: "Father, if it is at all possible, make this cup pass from me"[58]. Although he was Lord of things possible and impossible, by addressing the father he showed the consubstantial[59] Trinity, and at the same time the nature of his humanity which had been elevated[60] so greatly to the divinity. He prayed not for one people or one part, but for all men and the world — not only men, but for all living things on land, in the water, and in the air, on earth and in heaven. For although he was Son according to his divinity, yet through being clothed in a body[61] he learned from the torments of death the tribulation of all living things that had fallen under the corruption of death; in order that since they had been fully involved in the corruption of **[p. 254]** mortal creatures, he might be able to help them to impassibility. So the things that were impending were not small or insignificant, but greatly awesome.

For if at the death of Osea son of Amon, killed by guilty men, all Israel put on mourning, not one tribe or two but all, as the prophet greatly lamented: "In that day, he said, you will make great wailing like the lamentation of Adadroamtho in the plain, the tribe of the house of David apart, and their women apart, the tribes of the house of Nathan apart and their women apart, the tribes of the

[57] I.e., Gen. 3.7.

[58] Mt. 26.29; cf. Mk. 14.36, Lk. 22.42.

[59] Consubstantial: *miasnakan*, as also p. 308. See Thomson, *Teaching*, p. 13, for this and other terms used of the Trinity.

[60] Elevated: *veraberac'aw*. See the Introduction for Elishe's theology of the Incarnation.

[61] Clothed in a body: *marmnazgec'ik*. Cf. *sarkophoros*, used by Athanasius and Proclus of Constantinople; see Lampe, s.v. Equivalent expressions are common in the *Teaching*, see Thomson, p. 18-19.

house of Simon apart, and their women apart"[62] — how much more at the death of the Son of God was heaven humbled, the earth shaken, and all spiritual powers terrified!

Then the Lord of all in this place, not once only but two and three times, falls down, as if heaven fell to earth; and again stood up, as if raising the earth up with him and setting it up on high, making a unity of heavenly and earthly [things]. No light load was it to carry heaven and suspend the earth from himself. Do you see, no little sweat flowed from the divine body, but intense sweat and blood; and blood not in small quantity, but greatly-flowing rivers, whereby he sanctified heaven and illuminated earth, and purified the air from the former smoke of the fumes of the sacrifices of corruption.

Despite all these wondrous acts the disciples fell into profound slumber. Yet the benevolent Lord with gentle forbearance approached and woke the disciples, like the world from sleep, lamenting: "O Peter, were you thus unable to stay awake for a moment?[63] For in six days I made the heaven and earth and all its order, and now behold this is now six thousand years that they have been ruined, subject to corruption[64]. So then, wake up and stay awake for a little while, and throw off from yourself the heaviness of sleep, and see what your nation will do **[p. 255]** with me in return for all my good works up until today. How do they wish to repay me, all who have gathered as if against one condemned to death, not to put him to death according to the world's usual death, but with great indignities? I am greatly disturbed and mourn bitterly, because I know what will come to pass at my death. This chosen temple will be ruined; the priesthood will be

[62] Zech. 12.12-13.

[63] Mt. 26.40, etc.

[64] For the importance of the number six see the Introduction.

silenced; worship will cease; the readings of the holy testaments which cried out concerning it[65] will take on mourning; the continuous fire will be extinguished; the sacrifices will be suppressed; the holocausts for sin will cease; the making of vows from afar will be no more; the lovely city of Jerusalem will be destroyed, and all Israel will be scattered. Furthermore, you twelve who are with me will be scandalised this evening. Because it is written, it must be fulfilled: "I shall strike the shepherd, and the sheep will be scattered"[66]. But flocks without a shepherd are then betrayed into the hand of carnivorous wild beasts; especially because on this day they will have succeeded in sifting you like grain[67]. And I shall beg the Father that your faith be not weakened"[68].

Well did he say "that it be not weakened." For it is not the will of the divinity to see the wickedness of mankind; but it behooves man to put on virtue for the care of his soul, and to enter the kingdom and joy of the Father. "Let it not be weakened," he says, but not "lest you lose faith"[69]. To lose faith or not to lose faith was in his hands. Indeed that is to accept the task of loving-kindness. And just as he cried to the Father with mournful cry on behalf of all Israel: "Let not the chosen race perish,"[70] so also he entrusted the twelve to the holy Spirit, that they might stand firm in the hour of trial. Peter, in compassion for love of his Lord, was boastful through inexperience; but the Lord foretold to him what would occur. Peter, learning from the temptations, bitterly with great remorse set himself back to work. And he who in the time

65 It: *Vasn nora* refers to the temple and its worship.
66 Zech. 13.7.
67 Lk. 22.31.
68 Lk. 22.32.
69 Lose faith: *uranal*, perhaps "apostatise."
70 If this is a biblical phrase, I have not traced it.

of temptation was [**p. 256**] softer than wax, later appeared firmer than adamant.

Oh, how great was the insolence of the priests and the high-priest and all the magnates who were with them! While the Lord of all prayed on behalf of all, mourning lest they be betrayed into incurable torments, they paid no heed at all to what was about to happen, but even more arrogantly than the Sodomites moved to the attack. And truly did I say with still greater wickedness than they. For the angels gave no sign to Sodom[71], but they made Sodom a fearful sign to all onlookers, and worthily was retribution exacted on the unworthy. For if all parts of the land received divine torments for not honouring the angels, then, where the Lord of the angels endured the insults of death, who is capable of paying vengeance for that judgment? Not only did the solid[72] body in this visible [sphere] receive the sentence of death, but also the incorruptible spirit was bound up with the same body and cast into the undying fire of hell, which will burn with greater fierceness than the land of the Sodomites.

And the chief-priest and the crowd arrived, says [scripture], and without respect they seized and arrested Jesus; they bound him and led him to the house of the chief-priest. They bound him who came and unbound and loosed us from bonds. They led to the house him whom heaven and earth do not lead. The fiery nature entered and stood in the middle of the wooden house, and the house did not go up in smoke[73]. He who brought down fire onto their sacrifices and received them as expiation for sins, the

[71] Gen. ch. 19.

[72] Solid: *t'anjrac'eal,* contrasted with the spiritual, as p. 340. See further the Introduction for such vocabulary.

[73] Did not go up in smoke: *oč' caxer*; the verb is used of fire consuming an object.

same receiver stood before the sacrificing [priest], from whom Seraphim and Cherubim cover their feet and faces with their wings in awe of his greatnesss.

They demanded the Lord of the temple because of the temple. Oh enormous transgressions! What evil had he said? "Destroy this temple, and I shall [re-]build it on the third day"[74]. But we, they say, heard. Oh priests, so will this be a great transgression? They say, "Very great." **[p. 257]** "I shall build," he said, not "I shall destroy." It seems to me that you are not able to destroy in three days, and not even in many years. But he said well: "Tear down," because from the beginning you only know how to tear down and not to build. Behold, you destroyed[75] the nations of the just, but I shall build up other just ones among you. You also abolished prophecy from among yourselves, but I shall raise up other prophets to preach the truth to you. You dishonoured the stone which was the head of the corner[76], but I set up twelve stones in your land[77] so that I could build you up to an immovable foundation, and you did not wish it. So what is significant if you destroy your temple, and in three days I raise it up? Did I not set up heaven without [needing] a day, and establish earth without [needing] an hour, and arrange all existent things in six days? You built your temple over forty years; and I fashioned man in forty days in the womb[78]. You built your temple for forty years, and I instructed you for forty years in the desert, yet you were not instructed. So you who for forty years were not edified or

[74] Jn. 2.19.
[75] The following verbs are ambiguous; the 2nd. pl. aorist and 2nd. pl. imperative forms being identical.
[76] Mk. 12.10; Lk. 20.17.
[77] Josh. 4.3, etc.
[78] For the interpretations of forty see the Introduction.

instructed concerning the rock which gave you water in that same desert, you then destroy this temple which you see—[namely] me; and I on the third day will rebuild it without the work of hands. For if you wish to destroy another, you cannot. But this temple which Solomon built, whether you wish or not this will be destroyed by your enemies. Especially as my laments have been bitterly spoken over this temple. Just as you, O high-priest Caiaphas, prophesied [though] not of your own will: "Let the Romans come later, you said, and let them obliterate our nation and place and religion"[79]. Which will occur — not after many days, but you will see this in your own lifetime.

Saying this[80] and looking up even higher, he angered the high-priest and said: "I who now have entered and stand before you in bonds and great indignities you will see raised to heaven; and I shall sit on my Father's throne at the right hand of the hosts of God"[81]. When the high-priest heard this he grasped his collar and rent his robe in two[82]; **[p. 258]** for in the tearing of the robe he enrages the whole nation to rise up against Jesus. But perhaps you truly tore your robe because likewise the priesthood would be rent? For it was right to tear one's collar at the great evil which he was going to perpetrate at that place. The Lord's parables truly were most appropriate: "No one throws wine into old skins; otherwise the new wine splits the old skins"[83]. Into them trickled a little strong power, a little new wine, and then the old flasks split in two. But what great things did he say? He said the Son of Man

[79] Jn. 11.48.

[80] It is not entirely clear how much of the previous paragraph is meant to be a speech by Jesus, and how much the author's own rhetorical address.

[81] Cf. Mk. 14.62; Lk. 22.69.

[82] Mt. 26.65, Mk. 14.63. Cf. I Macc. 2.14, etc., for tearing one's collar as a sign of indignation or distress.

[83] Mt. 9.17; Mk. 2.22; Lk. 5.37.

would sit at the right hand of God[84]. O ancient blindness, those who do not all see even at their feet. The psalmist daily sings: "The Lord said to my Lord, sit at my right hand until I place your enemies as a stool for your feet"[85]. Not by raising up the one sitting does he order him to sit there, but he brings the format of sitting to making sit; nor does he repeat[86] the seated enemy by placing there those set in other form. He who was opposed like you he places as footstool to his feet. If it seems hard to you for a man to be the Son of God, why did you not previously tear [your robe] when you heard by the holy Spirit through Moses: "Release my elder son Israel that he may come and serve my cult. Otherwise I shall kill your elder son"[87]. So for your sake I wish that God kills the elder son of the king of the Egyptians, so that you may be the elder son of God. Yet you blaspheme and kill the only-begotten Son of God, and you are angry as to why he seats him at his right hand.

This opposition even surpasses the impieties of the demons and wages war at the same time against God and men and the holy Spirit. As the Lord said to me, "You see my son, today I have begotten you"[88]. Then he gives authority into his hands, not merely over the nation from which he was born, but over all Gentiles from the ends to the ends of the earth. So because you hated and rejected peace, **[p. 259]** gathering a crowd in general warfare against the earth — which previously you indicated by blowing the trumpet at the beginning of months and on your sabbaths,

[84] Mk. 14.62, Lk.22.69.

[85] Ps. 110.1.

[86] Repeat: or perhaps "bend down," *krknē*. The sense of this passage eludes me.

[87] Ex. 4.22-23.

[88] Heb. 5.5 = Ps. 2.7.

and at the full-moons and its waning, and on all your notable feasts — it is clear that from the beginning you had entered into battle against me. You who fought against all visible [things], against you all will join in battle. The trumpet will be silent, the sabbath be dissolved, the full-moons will appear to you in the land of the Gentiles, appearances of angels will no more occur for you. For all these had been poured upon you for honour and great glory. But the holy Spirit will depart and go from you, lest another prophet prophesy amongst you. Since you said he blaspehemed, and you dared to say this, everyone gave witness to your false words that he is guilty of death.

But on which guilty one, O accursed, do they inflict blows and spit in his face? You strike the one who adorned your head with precious stones, and you spit in the face[89] of him who at creation breathed into you a living spirit[90]. Concerning whom the blind man goes about crying openly through the streets of the city: "Whom they call Jesus, he made clay with his spittle and applied it to my eyes; he ordered [me] to wash in Siloah, and I see"[91]. The blind man received his sight, and you, seeing one, were blinded. Do you see that it was pride for the foolish and incomparable patience for God? By the impious he is beaten, and the liberator of all receives spit on his face from sinners. This is superior to human nature; he who made creatures, he alone could endure all this.

Again I ask you, O high-priest: Whence did you give the silver to the betrayer? Did I not previously tell you not to give? I never bought just blood for silver. Behold now you receive them both upon you.

[89] Mt. 26.67; cf. Mk. 14.65.
[90] Gen. 2.7.
[91] Jn. 9. 6-7.

When Judas saw that he had betrayed the Lord to judgement of death, he greatly repented; and he returned the silver to the high-priest and to the elders of the people, [**p. 260**] saying: "I sinned because I betrayed just blood." But they said: "It is no concern to us, you know [what to do]"[92]. He threw the silver into the temple, went off, hung himself, and died.

O Judas, how wicked it was for you to abandon your true teacher who taught you the paths of righteousness and words of truth. Who taught you the opposite confession? "I sinned, because I betrayed just blood." You were a disciple of the Son of Man, you learned the teaching from heaven and earth, you saw the miraculous operation of the holy Spirit, you knew him to be the Son of God. Yet now you say: "I sinned because I betrayed just blood." Which of the just ever rebuked the sea, and its waves ceased?[93] To which prophet were the demons ever subject, as to the name of Jesus Christ through the seventy?[94] Rather than saying; "I betrayed just blood," why did you not say: "I betrayed the Son of God?" Let Annas and Caiaphas be ashamed before the whole people. Rather than bringing your silver to the priests, why did you not bring it to Pilate? Rather than throwing it into the temple, why did you not throw it at your eternal judgment? Let the judge call all the honourable ones of the people, and reproach and reprimand the high-priests: "You sell the innocent man for money and condemn him with false words, and you make me a sharer in your impiety." Furthermore, rather than going home and hanging yourself, you should have run in person to the judge shrieking and raising a hubbub, declaring before all the multitude the great works and miracles which your teacher was doing. And

[92] Mt. 27.3-5.

[93] Mt. 8.24-26; cf. Mk. 4.39, Lk. 8.24.

[94] Lk. 10.17.

if even thus they would not listen to you, you should have stood before the cross and said in front of the crucified one: "I sinned because I betrayed just blood." He was the father of pity and lord of mercy, who did not come to judge men but to absolve and to pardon the transgressions of each one who turned to the crucified one. Your sins were not greater than the mercy of God, who in a loud voice cried out and said: "Everyone who is thirsty, let him come to me **[p. 261]** and let him drink living water from me,"[95] both for forgiveness and for immortality. Did he not pour his great blood on the ground for the great sins of the world, and by that holy blood redeem the dead and the living? Reckon that you were one of them. He who was able to do everything, for you only did you reckon him not sufficient for salvation? It is clear that the one who induced the first man to sin, the same clothed you with mole-like blindness; on your erring soul the ray of the grace of the Son of God did not shine. Therefore in vain were you striken, and you inherited suffocating bitterness.

Truly then the holy Spirit mourned, speaking from the mouth of David: "Be not silent, God of my blessing; for the mouth of a sinner, the mouth of a traitor was opened against me. They spoke of me with treacherous tongues, and surrounded me with words of hatred. They fought against me without cause, but I remained at prayer"[96]. So all this psalm was spoken with evil and curses against the betrayer, which with great endurance the Lord fulfilled at the crucifixion. Because he condemned to death the one innocent of sin, the saying was fulfilled against him: "Who will blaspheme the holy Spirit will not be forgiven in this world, nor in the future one"[97]. Just as indeed happened to him. For his fellow

[95] Jn. 7.37.

[96] Ps. 108.2-4.

[97] Mt. 12.31.

disciples were angry, and the priests were enraged, and his family rejected him. No one troubled to seek out his irreparable destruction, and no one brought him down from the cruel scaffold. His belly swelled and his guts flowed out, and all his bones were scattered in hell. Like a dog he died, and like carrion he was dragged out[98]. He departed destitute of works and his name was obliterated from the book of life.

Then the high-priests and elders of the people took the silver and said: "It is not right to keep this in the treasury, because it is the price of blood"[99]. They considered, and bought the potter's field. O great foolishness of the priests. Was it right to give that money from the temple, but not right to receive it [back]? Not now was that silver corrupted, but earlier by a long time, from the days of the prophet Jeremiah: **[p. 262]** "I took, he says, the thirty [pieces of] silver, the price of the one sold whom I bought from the sons of Israel; and I gave it as the price for a potter's field"[100]. For do not think that it is the view of a man, says the prophet: "Just as the Lord gave a command to me." Behold you appear to be offspring of Satan, for you continuously carry out the deeds of your father. So your silver is not corrupt, but you have corrupted the purity of your silver.

Foul was Goliath the Philistine[101], and through foul arms he wished to slaughter Israel. But God through David destroyed the pride of him in whom Satan dwelt, and through the weapon of the same he struck off the giant's head. The sword with which he

[98] Like a dog... out: as of Vasak in Elishe's *Armenian War*, p. 139-140.

[99] Mt. 27.6-7.

[100] Zech. [not Jeremiah!] 11.12-13. Ephrem, *Commentary*, XX 19, does not identify the author of this quotation.

[101] Philistine: *aylazgi*, "foreigner." The term is widely used in the Armenian OT for Philistines, and later for Muslims.

smote was not only not considered impure, but very holy indeed, and he gave it to Abiat'ar the high-priest[102]. He took it and placed it for safe-keeping under the altar, dedicating the victory to God and not to man. And the altar was not corrupted. Solomon built the temple not by [his own] power [but] with heathen revenues and with the help of Hiram the idolator[103], whence the cursed Jezebel led Israel astray[104]. Again, whence did Zorababel renew the temple's ornament, as is clear to all. For on their return they smote many nations, and with the booty of the captivity they put in order the ruin of the temple, which the great prophet Aggai clearly notes: "The glory of this house, he says, will be greater at the end than at the beginning"[105]. And lest they might reckon impure the booty of the fallen corpses, Zechariah said: "And there will be on that day on the bridles of the horses 'For the purity of the Lord'"[106]. Which was fulfilled in fact for Jerusalem when the 120,000 were struck in the days of Joshua, son of Yosedek the high priest, and of Zorababel, son of Salatiel[107].

So it is not that your silver is not worthy to be received into the treasury, but you should be expelled from the all-holy temple. Not only did you corrupt its silver, but also the laws of Moses by not accepting the fulfiller of the laws. Therefore not only the vessels of the temple accuse you, but also heaven and earth with all their adornment.

[p. 263] "They[108] led Jesus away in bonds from the house of Caiaphas to Pilate. And they did not enter inside lest they be

[102] For Goliath's sword cf. Ephrem, *Commentary*, XX 19.
[103] For Hiram and Solomon see III Kgs., ch.5.
[104] Ahab married Jezebel and was led into idolatry, III Kgs., ch. 16.
[105] Haggai 2.10.
[106] Zech. 14.20.
[107] Judges 8.10, Neh. 12.26.
[108] A, p. 243, begins the homily "On the Passion of Christ" here.

polluted"[109]. Where would your purity be, O priests? You polluted the holy temple with the price of the one sold; you polluted yourselves and all those close to you by the undertaking [to shed] holy blood. So why did you not enter into the tribunal? If that judgment occurs righteously, he is not found worthy of death, and you are saved by that just blood. But the place, whose floor those holy soles trod, if it previously had any stain of impiety, through that just judgment the whole house would have been purified and cleansed with the tribunal. So if you at all loathe the judge as an uncircumcised Gentile, behold he comes out to you; standing near you without intermediary he speaks with you, the supposedly holy high-priests. But it seems to me that the one you abhor previously realised not only your impurity but also your great impiety. For he knew that out of envy you handed him over. Wherefore he questioned you twice, thrice, and many times: "What evils has he committed that you bring him and hand him over to judgment of death?" But since they did not find at all an occasion for replying, they made him responsible for some great disturbance from Galilee as far as Jerusalem, and also calumniated him for royal [pretensions][110].

"When Pilate saw, says [scripture], that they were not entering, he himself went out to them"[111]. Condemning them in his mind, he said: "O, I know that you are priests and high-priests; you never can speak falsely because you are holy. You have never come inside to me lest you be polluted. So tell me, what evil deeds has he done, for you have abandoned the joy of your honourable feast, and like zealots of righteousness you seek vengeance as on an evil-doer. Give me in writing the charge against this man so

109 Jn. 18.28. Cf. Ephrem, *Commentary*, XX 15, and Lyonnet, p. 89.
110 Lk. 23.2-5.
111 Jn. 18.29.

that I may render justice according to his deeds." They all said together: **[p. 264]** "We know that he is guilty of death according to our law"[112]. The judge was angry and said: "It seems to me that you are persons hating the truth. How can I kill this innocent man without transgression? So take him and judge him according to your laws and as you are accustomed." The high-priests replied and said: "We have a command from our laws not to kill anyone"[113]. The judge said: "And I am afraid of the Roman laws to judge any just person without transgression." The high-priests said: "We bear witness that he is guilty of death, because he is a seditious man and promotes himself to royal status." Again the judge said: "What sort of seditious person? Is he a highwayman like a brigand, or tyrannical like a king, or a despoiler and plunderer? On what mountain did he live, and what roads did he frequent, and what travellers did he rob, and what province did he plunder? What did he carry off captive — men or animals? Bring a survivor of the company he captured, so that I may learn more of the truth from them. And if he seized anyone's treasures by force, why did you not protest to me before? If, as you say, he disturbs you by royal claims and takes from the taxes of the emperor, show me who his servants are, and how many soldiers he has, and what sort of armed equipment, whereby he is able to resist the Romans, removing you from subjection to the emperor, as you said."

When the priests saw that he had enclosed them on all sides and reduced them to inability to respond, they began with brazen faces to speak with the judge, and said: "O noble judge, why do you not believe us righteous ones? When you saw us in the court

[112] Jn. 19.7.
[113] Jn. 18.31.

it was not right for you to make many enquiries with such words, but merely to believe us and immediately carry out what we were saying." When Pilate heard this he condemned the foolishness of their replies, reprehending the high-priest in his mind. Then Pilate entered to Jesus and said: "Are you truly the king of the Jews?"[114] Jesus replied and said: "By your own word did you say that to me, or did someone else put the words into your mouth?" **[p. 265]** Pilate said: "I am not a Jew. Your fellow-countrymen delivered you into my hands. What did you do to them?" Jesus replied and said: "I am indeed a king, O judge, but not of this world." The judge said: "If that is so, you are some kind of king."

Then Pilate went out to the Jews and said to them: "You should all know that I cannot find a single reason for death against him. It is your custom that one of the prisoners be released on the feast. Do you wish that I should release for you this king of the Jews?" In unison they raised a cry and said: "Not him, not him, but release for us the son of Abba"[115]. Now this son of Abba was a brigand. When Pilate heard that, he was greatly saddened at the fury of the people. "In everything, he said, I see you erring from the truth. You make him guilty of disturbance, yet you could not bring a single charge of harm against him. You slandered him with the title of royalty, but you did not show me any act of authority. As for this brigand who over a long time has been committing many evils, who plagued the roads on the plain, slaughtered people, intercepted travellers, chased herdsmen from the mountains, was a highwayman on the roads, broke through the walls in settlements, took the treasures of the rich, mercilessly

[114] Jn. 18.33.

[115] Jn. 18.39-40. Elishe sometimes gives the form "Barabba," and sometimes "son [*ordi*] of Abba." Cf. Lyonnet, p. 88, for this rendering of the Syriac, not found in the Armenian bible.

made the poor lament, feared not God and was not ashamed of mankind, did not respect judges and flinched not from torture, paid no heed to fines, was involved in every impurity, commited all crimes, whom from a long time since I was seeking and scarcely arrested with great effort — now would it be right for you to request such a man on this feast?"

The high-priests responded and said: "Because this is a great feast, we wish that a great sinner be released on this great feast." Pilate replied to the high-priests and said: "Since you are so philanthropic and you seek the salvation of a great sinner on this great feast, I shall release Christ to you. As you said, he is the greatest sinner of all." On hearing this, they were all astonished and no response was found in their mouths. [**p. 266**] They stirred up the large crowd, cried out loudly and said: "Not him, not him, but release for us the son of Abba." Pilate spoke again: "But what shall I do with the king of the Jews?" They in the same tone said even more vehemently than before: "Remove him from us and crucify him"[116].

While the judge was still in the court his wife sent to him and said: "Have nothing to do with that just man, because many things have befallen me this night because of him"[117]. The judge sent [word] to his wife, saying: "But what shall I do? I can render account to the high-priests, and I can return a response to the priests. But the cry of the crowd I cannot withstand. Not only can I not help this man, but I am very frightened for myself, lest perchance I unwillingly become involved in just blood. You in your night vision were astonished, and I am intimidated at his righteousness. Indeed in the daytime I was awed by his face. For just as

[116] Jn. 19.15.
[117] Mt. 27.19.

a man is more than the shadow of his soul, that much more is the appearance of his sight than night-terrors."

Now when the judge saw that all the multitude were crying out in unison: "Crucify him,"[118] and that they were hurling against him even more words of blasphemy concerning the [accusation of] royalty, he immediately asked for water and washed his hands. And he removed himself from all the multitude of the court, saying in front of the priests and high-priests: "Know, O Jews, that I am innocent of this blood which you wish to shed unjustly." They in unison agreed: "His blood, they said, if it is of a just man is upon our heads; and if it is of a sinner, is on our heads and those of our children; and if it is of the Son of God, is on us and on our children and our children's children." Then he released to them Barabbas, the son of Abba, and he gave Jesus bound into their hands that they might crucify him[119].

O limitless benevolence of God and immeasurable greatness of his love which surpasses mind and thought — not only the understanding of mankind, **[p. 267]** but also that of the angels above. Everyone who ploughs the land breaks up the body of another and nourishes the outer growth of seeds. Now Jesus the heavenly one was made earth[120], and by his wish he came to ploughing and breaking up[121], and on his own body he took the seeds of all our wickedness. On his holy face he received the foul spit from obscene and blasphemous mouths. He who with his all-holy spittle opened the blind eyes of our bodies and souls[122],

[118] Mt. 27.23, etc.

[119] Mt. 27.23-26.

[120] Made earth: *erkrac'aw*. This seems to be a hapax in Armenian, but cf. the Greek *geinos* used by Gregory of Nyssa regarding Christ's birth, Lampe, s.v. See the Introduction for Elishe's terminology for the Incarnation.

[121] Cf. the common image of Christ as farmer, *georgos*, Lampe, s.v.

[122] Mk. 7.32, 8.23, Jn. 9.6.

received a buffeting from the servants of servants[123], and freed [us] from the buffeting of invisible torments. He who was free and the liberator of all, gave himself to blows that by his own freedom he might free us from the servitude to which we had willingly given ourselves in unworthy service. By the same will he had made not only the earth but also our bodies produce thorns, more especially the soul rather than the body. He pulled out by the roots the growth of our evil thorns; and he did not leave them on the ground, but formed them into a circle like an honourable crown, and it was placed on his head.

O how great is the wickedness of mankind and how great the benevolence of God! He who crowned the priests with gold and emeralds and many other precious stones, and adorned them in long robes[124] woven with gold, and the sound of bells and the wonderful amice; in return for all this I see perverse repayment. For not only did they put a crown of thorns on his head, but also a reed of derision in his right hand[125]. But I am particularly amazed at this — how it could be a reed of derision. It seems to me that not today did this reed grow, but from the day of Isaiah the prophet. "The very dim lamp, he said, will not be extinguished and the shattered reed will not be bent, until he brings to judgment the laws of righteousness"[126]. This is clear to all: by light the courts are directed, and by a reed writing is formed. Now if the very feeble lamp was John, as indeed truly he was, so far as they were able they hastened to extinguish it. But he more brightly than the rays of the sun sent forth the brilliance of his light. Well then do you fulfil the previously-written words of your

[123] Mt. 27.30.
[124] Long robes: *pčłnawor*, as Ex. 28.39, etc.
[125] Mt. 27.29.
[126] Is. 42.3.

prophets, but cruelly do you receive the sentence of judgment in yourselves. [**p. 268**] With a reed men are inscribed and released to freedom from cruel servitude. But behold, you with an earthly-grown reed are inscribed by the divine hand in indelible ink, and released from heavenly freedom to satanic servitude. So rightly then you take the reed from his hand and you strike his head, so that it may appear that you personally separate yourselves from that head which will crown all the saints with the unfading crown of the kingdom.

"Then, says [scripture], they offered him wine mixed with gall. He tasted and did not wish to drink"[127]. This seems to be an occasion for even greater love. As for the vine which he transferred from Egypt, he pulled up many vines in Canaan and [in their place] planted it[128], walled it around with the law, and fortified it with the prophets. He appointed for it kings as overseers, priests and high-priests as leaders, covenants and sacrifices, and divine oblations by day and by night. The lord of the vineyard came at the time of fruit to receive from them the pleasant taste of the vine. The wine did not change its sweet nature, because the divine right hand had planted the vineyard. They gave him to drink gall mixed into the wine. The gall is total bitterness. This is not the fruit of the divine plant, but the invention of evil-loving men and jealous desires, who wish to mix up the unmingled and wanted to mingle the bitterness of their own sins into the holy nature of God's work. This the divinity does not entrust to you, because not [only] did they mix a little gall, but they rendered it as thick as the prophet David had previously said in lament: "They provided gall for my food, and they gave me vinegar to drink"[129]. Since you are

[127] Mt. 27.34; but this is out of sequence. See below, p. 275.
[128] I.e. Israel as the [true] vine replaces the vines of Canaan.
[129] Ps. 69.21.

liberal in evils and restrained in beneficence, I shall not fulfil this desire of yours. He tasted and did not wish to drink. For they so wished that if it were possible he might consume much gall and drink even more vinegar. And if someone were to say: "Whence do you know unrevealed wishes, and especially unwritten ones," understand from their preparations. [**p. 269**] For whom among mankind indeed at the hour of his death were gall and vinegar ever provided for consolation, save only for those whose leader and teacher was their father Satan, those who with him are to inherit the place prepared for the two sides?[130]

So Barabba, whom they reckoned as very just, was graciously released to them by the judge. And two even more wicked brigands, whose deeds surpassed in wickedness and cruelty those of all the condemned to death who at that time were kept in the judge's prison, on the same day shared the crucifixion of Christ, one on his right and one on his left[131], so that not a single word of the previously written prophecy would fail.

There followed him a multitude of men and women, of priests and high-priests, interpreters of the law and elders of the people. They hastened to be eyewitnesses of the unworthy death of their life-giver. Great was the joy among those in error that he would be crucified among brigands, blasphemed on earth and condemned in heaven. For mankind has the natural habit that when they see someone in great misfortune and in cruel afflictions and in mockery of an unworthy death, they think in their impious minds that punishment from God has fallen upon him. They become very angry, and endeavour out of their own cruelty to increase even more the tortures of those being punished. This thoughtlessness is

[130] But different places were prepared for the two sides according to Mt. ch. 25!
[131] Mt. 27.38; not John.

the product of a blind mind which merely understands what is present and does not see the future, which has fallen away from the truth and has lost the life to come. As indeed happened at the place that provided salvation — the choice of the two sides, some falling down and some to rise up. For while they were eager to blaspheme and quick-sighted to mock his indignities, they wished to hear also insults of him from the mouth of the brigands. For when a man is cruelly cast into harsh torments and has despaired of his life, is close to the gate of death from which there is no return — especially such a death [p. 270] in which the brigands were placed — such a man is not ashamed to insult his judge and even to raise the words of his blasphemy to heaven.

But come now, come up to the luminous spot and approach the saving cross of the Lord, and see the new and incomparable works that have been effected. Three wooden [crosses] were set up and three men crucified, all in a common punishment, no one of them in an easier position but each of them in very cruel torment. In that place I am greatly astonished as to how the robber became an advocate of the truth. He looked with clear eye and [saw] nothing surprising. Previously he did not know the true teaching of the Lord. By his own deeds he was empty of just works. Heavenly wisdom was far from him, because he was the offspring of sin and the product of bitterness, a man who from his youth like a madman has escaped from the city to the countryside, had removed himself from mankind, hated the light of day and loved the darkness of night, was an accomplice of city robbers and a partner of thieving brigands. His thoughts were deceitful and his acts wicked; he was a friend of the unworthy and dear to the licentious, a hater of the prudent and execrated by all men who love the good. Hunted down by the judge, he was seized for his many transgressions; and for those many transgressions he was inflicted with mortal punishment. What then does he say? Rebuking his companion and condemning himself, he casts invective on the priests and even more on the high-priests. It seems to me that he greatly blames the judge, and at the same time upbraids the court and shames the wise colleagues of the judge.

His companion was a fellow of the blasphemous people[132], and he began to mock and say: "If you are really the Christ, save yourself and us with you." But the other in a loud voice, in the hearing of all the people, began to quarrel with his companion and say: "Are you not afraid of God? Likewise, you should be put to shame by men. We have received retribution as a consequence of our perverse behaviour, but why this one? For he has done nothing wicked and has never wronged any man." **[p. 271]** By saying this he put to shame all the multitude of condemners. Then addressing his words to that same person, the brigand said: "Lord Jesus, remember me at the coming of your kingdom"[133]. I do not know the name of this man, yet I am ashamed to call him a brigand, for he became superior not only to any doer of good among men, but also to those most learned in the law and the prophets.

What prompted you to this, O robber? Where are you, whom do you see, with whom do you speak? On a cross you see one crucified, and you speak with the Lord Jesus, and at the same time with the son of the king who rules over the kingdom and distributes gifts to all. So then what did you see? Surely not that he softened the wood of his own cross more than that of yours. Do you not see the four-angled[134] wood set up on the rock, the feet and

[132] See Lk. 23.39ff; not Mt. 27.44.

[133] Lk. 23.42.

[134] Four-angled: *č'orek'kusi,* lit. "foursided." For parallels with the extended exegesis of the four points of the cross in the *Teaching* and other texts see the Introduction.

hands nailed with iron, bound with indissoluble bonds? The spearmen surround him, the priests blaspheme, the high-priests condemn, the elders mock insolently, the Pharisees trample unblushingly. The multitude of the people cry out in a loud voice: "He saved others, himself he cannot save"[135]. You yourself see the reed of mockery and the vinegar mixed with gall for food and drink; the clothes stripped off, the robe cast for lots, the naked [body] hanging on the cross, the head crowned with thorns, the face filled with spit, the cheeks buffeted. And you say: "Remember me at the coming of your kingdom"[136].

I am greatly amazed as to whence shone such a light on the soul of the brigand, and even more than greatly astonished. He had not gone to Nazareth, he was not informed about his birth, he had not gone to Cana of Galilee, no one had summoned him to the wedding, he had not drunk of the wine that flowed from the jar[137], he had not seen the blind man annointed with clay[138], he had not learned from the Samaritan woman[139], he had not seen the couch of the paralytic[140], he had not gone to the empty tomb of Lazarus[141], he had not heard the protest of the demons in the land of the Gergesenes[142] — why should I enumerate each one individually? **[p. 272]** Just as his soul was devoid of good works, so he had not seen or heard any of the miracles performed by our Lord. So instead of all these glories he saw a man full of dishonour at the death of the cross, yet he confessed him [to be] Lord

135 Mt. 27.42; cf. Lk. 23.35.
136 Lk. 23.42.
137 Jn. 2.8.
138 Jn. 9.6.
139 Jn. 4.7.
140 Mk. 2.5.
141 Jn. 11.38.
142 Mt. 8.29.

Jesus, Son of God, and ruler of the kingdom of the Father's glory. Undoubting faith, fully-believing queries! Therefore he heard a truthful response: "Verily I say to you, today you will be with me in paradise"[143]. Brief questions, comprehensive reply! Through the word of faith he heard the word of the Word's reply. What could he do in that situation? He poured his whole self out before the Lord of all as a man and poor, but only made great through faith. But the Lord, not as a man and not as poor and envious, and not as parsimonious, but as a beneficent liberal rich man with noble intention grants not a part of the gift but the entire original ancestral place — not where the tree of death was, but where was only the tree of life. Not the unfenced place where the serpent crawled and entered, but which God himself had barricaded with the sharp point of a lance in a fiery circle which the cherubim guarded, the fence of which none of the just could breach — not Abraham, not Isaac, not Jacob, not even Moses with the law nor the prophets with their preaching, not the priests with their sacrifices nor the Levites in their worship, not those who took a vow among those dedicated, not the true father nor just kings, not the groups of martyrs nor the ranks of apostles, especially were I to speak in higher terms — not angels nor archangels, nor thrones nor principalities, not lordships nor powers were able to open the gate of paradise, but only that brigand.

Rightly was it said that the brigand opened the gate of paradise, because at that hour all creatures were in sad mourning. The sun was hidden, the moon was darkened, the stars were obscured, the daylight departed and night drew near; those on high were astounded and those below bewildered; the disciples fled **[p. 273]** and acquaintances went afar off, friends [became]

[143] Lk. 23.43.

slanderers, relatives enemies. All abandoned [Jesus], standing completely to the rear; only he drew near to confess. He did not make a beginning from his birth, nor from particular miracles did he comprehend. But he was raised up in suffering form, and he reached the invisible kingdom and said: "Remember me in the kingdom that has no torments at your coming."

What would be that coming, or whence would he come, and for whose purposes would he come? And how did you know, O brigand? Tell us. Since you became a companion of Moses, behold you were raised up higher than Sinai, and you saw an incorporeal vision. It seems to me that the holy Spirit encountered you, and you saw the Father of all. And those prepared gifts which the great Paul was unable to interpret for us, you previously entered and inherited.

"Yes, he said, this is true. Because the Lord himself led me; and he has promised even more. Not only did he send me to paradise lest the serpent remove me thence again; but for that reason he said: "You will be with me within paradise." By saying "with me" [he means] not temporally nor eternally, but absolutely continuously — God himself is always with himself, God is with the perpetual believer.

Therefore he came to torments so that he might be of assistance to the one in torment. The first fruit of the first tree killed the first man; but the first fruit of the cross killed the leader of death in his own person; and on the death of death the first fruit, the brigand, was plucked by the power of the cross. O evilly-demonic priests, will you still mock the cross or laugh at the one crucified? While you were wishing to kill him among the impious, by the impious one you pious ones were reproved and admonished. And the impious one became superior to the pious ones — not only to you, but also completely superior to your law.

Why then was this so? For the law was not weak at all, but you made it weak by not observing the law because you were without faith. [p. 274] But he with faith saw the law and the legislator. He saw that the law was lacking in faith and could not be found. He saw that the legislator had come to fulfil the law and not to make it less. At the same time he advanced and honoured the law with faith, because he confessed the giver of the law. He also honoured the legislator, because he said to him: God and Son of God, distributor of gifts and lord of the kingdom. He became the beginning of faith and the fulfiller of the law, son of Abraham and friend of the prophets, a fellow-disciple of the apostles, leader of the martyrs, inheritor of the kingdom, gate-keeper of the garden of life, at once loving and beloved by the Father and Son and holy Spirit.

Now very dear to me is the saying of the Apostle: "Where there was especially sin, [there] especially was the grace of God"[144]. On hearing this, brethren, the minds of us all with true knowledge hasten to the visionary nation, to the offspring of the just, to the land of gifts, to the desirable city of Jerusalem, to the wonderful temple of God, where [are] the law given by God and the inspired prophets, the just are filled with grace, fathers made perfect and sons instructed, where [occurred] heavenly signs and earthly miracles, where [were] revelations of angels and the acceptance of offerings through the living holy Spirit, whereby God is truly known to those whose souls through holiness are made comparable with God. So because of all this I greatly love the land, and in the land the province, and in the province the chosen city, and in the city the elevated place Golgotha, and in that place the even higher rock, and on the rock the world-shaped[145] cross, and on the

[144] Rom. 5.20.

[145] World-shaped: *ašxarhajew*, i.e. with four extremities. See above, p. 271, for the elaborate exegesis of this theme in Armenian.

cross the one crucified, who hung in front of the heavenly onlookers, and yet was still above not only the heights of mountains but even heaven. He was raised even higher than the heaven of heavens.

Because this is so, look at the place and see the true accomplishment of deeds which were done there without doubt. For they stripped the Lord of creatures, the one who had clothed heaven with the adornment of light **[p. 275]** and had crowned the earth with sweet-smelling flowers. They cast lots for that robe which without measure or lot he had given to the sons of men as a garment of adornment by sea and dry land. In his thirst they did not give water to drink to the one who irrigated the whole face of the earth by the great downpour of the clouds in their abundant torrents, until he said in his torments: "I am thirsty"[146]. The establisher of fountains said: "I am thirsty." The lord of the Ocean and the giver of rains, lacking nothing and provider to the needy, said: "I am thirsty." The one who at the beginning of creation made creatures so watery[147] that the holy Spirit moved over the waters, and across great abysses made flow down such a depth of seas, the Lord of all this in loving mercy came to his own, but by his own was greatly tormented and subjected to torments so that he needed a single cup of water. Yet even though he said: "I am thirsty," no one gave him anything to drink[148].

O embittered hearts and corrupted minds and mad persons! For if anyone among us today had a feeling of heavenly love and ardour of the same desire, we too would say with him: "We are

[146] Jn. 19.28; in this first quotation the 1st p.s. pronoun *es* is added to the verb *em*.

[147] Watery: *jrayełc'*, "overflowing with water."

[148] But Mt. 27.48 and Jn. 19.29 refer to the sponge of vinegar; cf. Diatessaron, LII, 1-3, and p. 268 above.

thirsty," sharing in the pain of his great torments. Not that we might drink wine for the consolation of grief, but that willingly and despite the pain we might take upon ourselves the death and derision of the Saviour and run a brave course with endurance with a view to heroism, and raising the trophy[149] we might defeat the enemy. And we also shall lack a single cup of water for consoling thirst. Furthermore, the worthy lovers of Christ must share in the words of the prophet: "Someone took and made my head a store of many waters, and my eyes a source for abundant tears"[150]. And what did you do with all this, O prophet? "Day and night I wept for Israel." So he who in the fearful desert made abundant streams flow from the arid rock[151], the same without trouble for them followed the people to give drink to the chosen race. Now the same rock, for their sake also having become man here, said: "I am thirsty." Not only because they did not give him water, but even instead of water they offered him vinegar mixed with gall. **[p. 276]** Now what man would have such a stony heart or bronze body, that on hearing this he could hold back tears? For at the separation of our dear ones we tear [our faces] and lament[152]; we burn and seethe in compassion for our friends, and in accordance with the parts of the body we raise our voices in bitter laments. By doing this we do not do what is worthy, because we compensate for our guilt. Not because he himself is guilty, but that he might compensate for our guilt through his own. And not because he cried out to be spared from the debts, but being very dry and

149 Trophy: *axoyean*, not in Paul's epistles, of which the preceding phrases are reminiscent, e.g. II Tim., 4.7.

150 Jer. 9.1.

151 Ex. 17.6. For this common parallel between Christ and the rock see Lampe, s.v. *petra*.

152 Tear: *c'timk'*. A curious reminiscence of ancient practice forbidden by ecclesiastical authorities; cf. *Buzandaran*, V 31.

athirst, he asked for a little water to moisten his arid palate. He said: "I am thirsty." He did not call on anyone in person, he did not speak the name of any individual. He made his supplication to us, he revealed his need to all, he saw mercilessness in everyone.

I am unable to describe the crushed heart, the choking soul, the grieving mind, and the emotions of Mary. For while the Lord was in extreme torment they stood near him, says [scripture], his mother and his mother's sister Mary Magdalene[153], and other women who had earlier believed in the coming of the Son of God. With their own eyes they saw the great sufferings, and with their own ears they heard the blasphemies; especially when they heard from his mouth: "I am thirsty." You yourselves know the natural character of women, how tenderly inclined they are to compassion, and especially towards their own dear offspring. So what must one think at that moment about these women? For if they had found the means, not only would they have offered him water in a vessel, but they would have directed bountiful torrents around the cross. But since it was not in their capacity to do so, they beat their breasts, broke their hearts, grieved in their minds, and shed copious tears; they lamented for themselves and preferred death to life. While still in this world, they resembled stricken corpses. Concerning all this they had earlier heard a declaration from the Lord, who in lament spoke concerning the whole nation: "Daughters of Jerusalem, do not weep over me, but weep over yourselves and your sons and daughters. **[p. 277]** For the days will come in which they will say: Blessed are the barren, and the entrails which have not given birth, and the breasts which have not given suck. At that time they will begin to say to the

[153] Jn. 19.25 distinguishes Mary Madgalene from this Mary, the aunt of Jesus. See Lyonnet, p. 75, n.3 on this passage.

mountains: Fall on us, and to the hills: Cover us[154]. For if they did this to green wood, what will they do to the dry?"[155]

Then at that place was verified the prediction of the prophet Zechariah, son of Barek'; and the death of the son of Amon resembled the death of the Son of God. For this Osias was a just man and king of Israel; he led the people on paths of piety and never wronged any of mankind. By exhortation he brought the hearts of every man to the sole worship of God. While he was still completing his life in peaceable conduct, there came against him Pharaoh the Lame from the land of Egypt; he waged war with him and killed him in the land of Judaea[156]. Because the reign of Osia was truly just, and he was an only child from birth, and had vainly died in battle, the prophet was moved to compassion at the king's death, and exhorting the whole tribe he brought them to mourning and tears. He likens the severity of the mourning to pomegranate-trees cut down on the plain[157]. It seems to me that the flower of the pomegranate-tree is desirable and pleasant in men's eyes. But at the blowing of the hot wind it easily falls and droops down completely. That which previously was the most glorious of all flowers, later becomes more grievous and sad than all thorny trees. Therefore the prophet likened the just king to a flower and a crown; the people remained void and empty like trees without fruit, which appear useless to the sight of men.

So through the tribes four in number which the prophet brought to mourn the king, the men separately and the women separately, he made the whole, soul and body, to mourn the king,

[154] A, p. 255, "On the Passion of Christ" ends here.

[155] Lk. 23.28-30.

[156] Cf. II Chron. 35.20. But the Armenian version has no reference to a "lame" [*kał*] Pharaoh.

[157] I.e. Megiddo, where Josiah was slain; Zech. 12.11-14. See also p. 254 above.

just as our Lord by saying to the women: "Daughters of Jerusalem," also indicated to them that they would lament over themselves and over all Israel — not only men and women separately, as [over] the house of David **[p. 278]** and of his three companions[158], but all nations and peoples, not only of mankind but also of the upper powers, as of heaven and of the heavenly ones. And they are of that number, and through the four they all mourn.

Why then would this be? Because they were all found in pitilessness. The Jews in vain condemned him and handed him over. Consequently the two sides were united in evil. Through the four elements by the four parts, the four corners in this world[159], the whole earth will lament together in great awe and fearsome mourning, the men separately and the women separately. Israel will lament because it was separated from the true God. The heathen lament because they are cut off from their fallen gods. The two sides embark on grief and great mourning. The lament of some turns to irreparable destruction, and of others from destruction to eternal light. In this place is truly fulfilled the saying of the prophet: "All the nations will mourn separately"[160]. Likewise there by the cross of the Lord not small and insignificant was the lamentation, but very great and fearsome, which surpassed all mourning.

[158] I.e. the other three tribes of Zech. 12.12-13.

[159] See also p. 271.

[160] Zech. 12.10.

[*On the Crucifixion*][1]

[p. 278] "At that same time, says [scripture], our Lord was raised up onto the cross. The sun grew dark, the veil of the temple was split to the bottom, the earth shook, rocks were rent, tombs opened, and many of the dead arose and after the resurrection of the Lord entered the holy city and appeared to many"[2].

So why was the sun hidden and the beautiful light of daytime lost, and darkness grew dense and thick over the earth? It is clear, and we cannot hide the truth. Because they stripped off his garments and took them for themselves, and they pinioned and nailed him naked to the wood, the upper hosts[3] were not able to look on the nakedness of the Lord of heaven and earth. The seraphim, who before the crucifixion surrounded his divinity, were unable to gaze on his awesome glory, but with two wings hid their faces, and with two wings hid their feet, and with two wings raised themselves and rose up, suspended around his invincible power. [p. 279] With fiery mouths they unceasingly said: "Holy, holy, holy," and with tireless voices praised his creative power[4].

[1] There is no new title in the text, but the editors here begin a new running header with this phrase. A, p. 256, begins with this title.

[2] Mt. 27.51-52, Lk. 23.45. For the conflation see Lyonnet, p. 90; cf. Ephrem, *Commentary*, XXI, 4-5.

[3] Hosts: *gundk'* is an ambiguous term, referring either to the spheres which carry the planets, or to companies of soldiers — here angels.

[4] Is. 62; Rev. 4.8.

Similarly the angels and archangels and all the ranks of the "vigilant"[5] ones stood in awe and trembling. They were unable to look and see his self-existent nature. They withdrew, avoided, and fled from the unapproachable rays of his natural self-produced light[6]. Not only honouring his creative power, but also knowing their own constraint, they did not dare to gaze on him boldly, to approach and draw near, lest they be destroyed and consumed by his inaccessible power. This is the concern of the Creator of all, to keep his creatures unharmed in each one's nature. Especially at the time when the awesome death of the Son of God appeared to those above and those below, the elements ministered to the honour of the crucified one and the concealment of the angels who did not wish to see and view the dishonour of his death. At the same time, shunning the foolish people who without shame or respect looked on the nakedness of the Son of God, darkness was distilled and became thick over their impudent faces. For they were unworthy to look on and see their own life on the cross.

Now Moses, having previously seen this example[7] through the Spirit of God, set up in the desert a court of judgment. For with regard to the saving beneficence of God to the people they were found not thankful, but blasphemers and complainers against Moses and against God. They angered and embittered the holy Spirit of God, so God sent against them deadly snakes; without mercy they struck and killed many of the people[8]. Then God in

[5] Vigilant: *zuart'un*, a common title for angels; cf. Syriac *'ira*, Greek *egregoros*. See also p. 350 below.

[6] Self-existent: *ink'nagoy*; self-produced: *ink'nacag*. For these terms see the Introduction.

[7] Example: *awrinak*, standard Armenian for "type."

[8] Num. 21.5-9. For the parallel of the snake and Christ see Lampe, s.v. *ophis* 5. It does not appear in the *Teaching*, and is discussed only briefly in Ephrem, XVI, 15.

his benevolence remembered the covenant which had been made with his beloved ones; he had pity and compassion for those struck and bitten by the snakes' attacks. He commanded Moses to make an artificial snake and to raise it on high among the people, so that whoever could look and see the snake of Moses would be able to survive the cruel poison of the murderous snakes. This is a very marvellous and spiritual sight. **[p. 280]** He commands Moses to make a snake, yet he does not suggest the name of the material[9], nor anything which is subject to the craftsman's hammer or of the other manufacturing arts which is formed without the essay of fire. But he only gave a command: "Make for yourself, he says, a snake." Make it yourself, he says. Looking to this, Moses was greatly enlightened; he saw the hidden [nature] of things to come and made a bronze snake. As it seems to me, in brief, as an obscure revelation of wisdom, Moses likened the invincible grace of God to bronze, so that those who had acquired it through true faith in the truth might be preserved unharmed. But he constituted the form of the bronze snake not in any other model but that of poisonous and mortal [snakes].

So see the nicety of the distinction. They were all struck but they did not all die, as the distinction of the judgment is clear. Since from gluttony[10] sin had entered the world through the intermediary of the first snake, the same desire for food moved the bodies of the insatiable people, whence was formed the blasphemous complaint in their mouths. They were struck and bitten by snakes, which brought death upon them. For there is nothing so similar to desire as the cunning and deceitful nature of a snake. It

[9] I.e. Elishe is separating God's command in v.8 from the action of Moses in v. 9.

[10] For gluttony leading to sin cf. Elishe, *Homily on the Transfiguration*, p. 239.

crawls and worms its way into narrow and slim crevices[11], it enters and demonstrates the act of cruel death. As female desire flows over and spills in the desire for food, it is moved and abandons itself to insatiable drinking, whence the many-headed beast, desire, is strengthened against the senses of man and drives his insatiability to obscene deeds.

Furthermore, the form of the snake's movement truly indicates the movements of our nature, just as we have learned from the scientists[12] who unerringly give confidence to philosophical men. The snake makes five windings in its crawling. The first ones and the next complete the seventh number, and [the latter] introduces the likeness of our senses: two eyes and equal ears, taste, understanding, and the lower belly[13] of the stomach, which moves every man to bodily desires. **[p. 281]** This is the downpour of snakes onto the concupiscent people, which through all forms of the senses were moved to desire and actually carried out their impure wishes.

At the smiting of the snakes they perished by death. And the one who was only trampled by the movements of desires, he was bitten by the poisonous snakes but did not become subject to death. You can look and see the snake of Moses, because it was a snake who killed; and the one who killed, the same also bit. And through the sight of the other snake, those who were bitten received healing. Those who were bitten and those who bit surrounded the snake raised up; and it was intermediary and judge

[11] Cf. Philo, *In Gen.*, I 31 ff, II 57.

[12] Scientists: *bnakan ark'*, lit. "physicists." The phrase is common in the Armenian version of Philo.

[13] Belly: *hamk'*, the singular meaning "savour." Elishe gives a different interpretation of the seven senses on p. 321. For his number symbolism see the Introduction.

for the two sides. It granted to some healing of life, and to others the opposite. The snake of bronze which was formed by the hands of the wise Moses was large; but the greatness of its power bore the likeness of the cross raised up, which was set up on Golgotha, which the Lord himself had previously ordained by saying: "Just as Moses raised up the snake in the desert, likewise the Son of Man must be raised up between the two sides, for some to irrevocable error, but for others to the path of truth"[14].

Now the sun was darkened over those gone astray, because they were not worthy to see the sun of righteousness which healed the wounds of the invisible first snake. Just as in the desert those who were struck in their souls by the snake of desire, [which] through their bodies performed acts of corruption, were not able to see the snake of Moses because they were not worthy of grace-given forgiveness, and so falling in their deaths they were stretched dead in the desert — but where a few, though affected by lustful desires, yet came to an easier healing — likewise here too, at the summit of this spot, the impious and the lawful, the unworthy and the worthy surrounded the cross of Christ. Those who were smitten with blindnesses of old were not able to see death returning to life, error turning into truth, and curses changing into blessing. **[p. 282]** They saw the immediate tribulations and were deprived of the future repose.

But he in accordance with his own benevolence granted the health of healing to both sides who had been bitten and wounded by the poisons of the old serpent[15]. And he granted health through their faith's eye to those who could look and see the Son of Man on the cross, who accepted torments in his own body, and would

[14] Jn. 3.14-15, somewhat expanded!

[15] Serpent: here *vishap*, as Ex. 7.9-12 of Aaron's rod, not *awj*, rendered as "snake" above.

understand the same [to be] the Son of God, creator of things visible and invisible. For he is not at all like the bronze snake of Moses which hung on wood in the desert, which for some was strong for healing but for others was weak to the irrevocability of death. For our Lord mentioned the likeness but not the nature of the likeness, which did not carry the reality of the truth. For if it had borne it, what need would there have been for the second to come in its place, as our great Apostle interprets for us the power of the crucified one: "The one who did not know sin, he says, for our sake became sin, so that we might become through him righteousness of God"[16]. And sin entered the world through the snake.

Now the Lord formed himself in the likeness of the snake; he was typified and took form in the seven senses and the indivisible separate intelligence. And they became sin, because we all under the same sin had been bitten and were biters: bitten by the first old poison of the serpent, and bitten by each movement of the written number of the parts of the body. Our eyes had been pierced by looking at unworthy things; our ears had been affected by hearing dissolute things, our taste by insatiable desire, and our movements by beastly lusts; and our intellect had been proudly raised up. We had become totally [wicked], and not one part of righteousness [was in us]. Yet he who did not know sin and is far from all this, through the will of his own benevolence became our sin, which was not his own, so that we might become righteousness through him. He who was ours we lost, but we shall be found through him lest we be lost again.

But this is the snake of bronze which Moses raised up **[p. 283]** in the desert. It does not know how to strike because it does not have poison in its nature. But it is not struck by others, because its

[16] II Cor. 5.21.

essence[17] is incomprehensible. Those smitten and the smiters surrounded it, so that their poisons might be cancelled by the invincible power of the essence of that body. And this snake was suspended on wood raised up, and not in an invisible and hidden place but on a very high hill. It was not hidden and covered by clothes, but naked in all its parts it was visible amidst the crowd of the people. It was clear to all, yet not all saw it. Those who saw received healing, and those who did not see were separated from this world and from the world of life.

So then truly our Lord likens to this snake not any of the just, and not any of the prophets, and not any of the perfect fathers[18], but a certain man alone and very isolated[19] — not an insignificant one, but the Son of Man who has the nature of us all and is superior to all, the Creator of all and the Renewer of everything, who has his body bitten but is not a biter; he is bitten in the body, but not in the soul[20]. I said body, in hands and feet, in ribs and back, in cheeks and head. Now his senses have the form of our number, but they are not smitten in our likeness.

Likewise I shall abbreviate in a few words: Men sin through the eyes before [sinning] by deed. But our Lord Christ looked with his eyes at the woman who was more sinful that the whole city in which she dwelt. He recognised her and made himself known to her. Eyes met eyes, and they poured out abundant tears in repentance. Sin died and righteousness came alive. Through their ears men were enslaved to lascivious songs. With the same ears our Lord entered the house of the high-priest and saw there death

[17] Essence: *goyac'ut'iwn*, cf. p. 243 above.

[18] Perfect: *katareloc'*, or perhaps "dead, martyred."

[19] Man: The Armenian has a dative case, which grammatically makes no sense.

[20] Soul: [*h*]*ogi*, or "spirit."

reigning. He heard the voices of lamentation and of great mourning. He expelled death and silenced the laments of mourning with despair. He also had the faculty of taste, but only that of the necessary things [**p. 284**] and not of the superfluous. He filled the needs of many, and the backs of those carrying loads were weighed down with brimful baskets. Through his faculty of intelligence he spoke with his Father on high, and on earth moved among men with graceful humility.

Since this is true in this fashion, I am not at all mistaken in saying that our body was found superior to our nature. Therefore he likens himself to the bronze snake as to sin and righteousness. To sin, because he appeared in accordance with our essence[21]; but to righteousness, because he did not move in accordance with our senses. Through all this he cast his hearers into a perplexity of doubt. "Just as Moses, he said, raised the snake in the desert, so it is necessary for the Son of Man to be raised up"[22].

With respect to what did the Lord say such words, they say, who was God by nature and also true man? Why did he who is Creator in his divinity and just in his humanity liken himself to a snake? O wise listener, that which was well said by the Lord do not understand as something confused and ugly. He likened himself to a snake, not to the one that bites and strikes, but to the non-poisonous and healing one. For by the poisonous snake we were smitten and died; but through the non-poisonous snake we were healed and cured. So the body is the essence of the snake, the body is also our nature. Body met body in paradise. Body spoke with body, body was deceived by body, and the poisonous one struck and killed the non-poisonous. Our Lord Jesus Christ took

[21] Essence: *goyac'ut'iwn*, as above, rather than *bnut'iwn*, the regular term for "nature" [as in the next paragraph].

[22] Jn. 3.14.

a body, not that of the poisonous old snake, but that of those wounded; and he made it mortal. Body appeared to body, the non-poisonous to the poisonous, the unharmed to the harmed, the impassible to the one tormented, the incorruptible to the corruptible. Behold, here once and for all I shall say: the immortal to the mortal, and God to man. He took on existence[23], and was contained in a corporeal body[24], and was suspended on the cross, not in the desert and not in a city, but outside a city and far from a desert.

All lands and cities gathered around him and all looked on, but not all saw. [**p. 285**] For those who saw, the poison of snake-bite dissipated, and without medicine they received perfect health. Eyes recovered by looking humbly and seeing the divinity in the guilty body; and through their ears they heard the same voice of the divinity which said: "Father, into your hands I place my soul"[25]. The discriminating taste was sweetened in the palate of those who heard the voice; and it filled them more than all the tastes of sweet food. Through their bodily senses their souls were made healthy, their minds were illuminated, and they became very clear-sighted. They looked at the sufferings of the cross, and they saw the impassible divinity of the Son; their faith was lifted up on wings[26] and reached the Father of all. They recalled Moses and the bronze snake, which was an exemplar of the new time that was fulfilled at the crucifixion of Christ. Not all were able to see. Those whose hearts were darkened and whose souls were dimmed in blindness of old, who had been affected by bodily

[23] Took on existence: *goyac'eal*. See the Introduction for this term.

[24] Corporeal: *t'anjrac'eal*, lit. "made solid." See the Introduction for the term.

[25] Lk. 23.46; but *dnem*, "place," for *awandem*, "commend;" cf. Ps. 30.6.

[26] On wings: lit. "flying."

desire and had wasted in their bodies, these stumbled and shook on the rock of foundation. From their eyes was held back the sight of the rays of light, of the brilliant cross of Christ which shone out amidst all creatures.

Therefore there appeared in that spot fearsome deeds and great and marvellous works. For the curtain which Moses had made by God's command and had drawn inside the temple to be an intermediary[27], keeping the holy of holies out of sight, [and] the outer temple in which the Levites continually performed their worship, bore the likeness of the heaven of heavens in which we suppose the nature of the uncreated [resides]. So what further need was there of the curtain which kept hidden the holy of holies, the mystery of the invisible power? But today it did not indicate the mystery but the real lord of the mystery, he who came to reveal and indicate the mystery as temporal help[28] so that they might recognise and receive the timeless lord of the mystery. But they not only did not receive him **[p. 286]** but even nailed him naked to the cross in death. Therefore the curtain was rent[29]. For at the rending of the curtain the holy of holies remained empty and void, because the holy Spirit had left the temple. And in return for not rending their garments over the [sheddings] of blood which they had worked, the curtain rent its collar over its Lord, who kept the mystery of its honour. At the rending of the curtain the hearts of the high-priests will be rent, when they will see the honour of the holiness which was torn in two; and they will be ashamed before all the people that they did not cast hands on a man but on the Lord of the temple. Just as the curtain was rent,

[27] Intermediary: *mijnord*, perhaps here "barrier." This is not the exegesis of Ephrem, *Commentary*, XXI, 4-6.

[28] I.e. as a help in the temporal world to understand the true reality.

[29] Lk. 23.45.

showing that "henceforth I am not at all necessary to hide the meagre holy things in which there will no longer be heavenly power, because they have been separated and removed from the Lord of heaven and earth" — likewise the earth moved beneath its inhabitants, the lawless people. Because the sun is a part of heaven, with the one part which cut off its light from creatures all parts of heaven trembled with it and put on mourning. And because the curtain is a part of the fruits of this earth, with the one part all parts of this earth trembled and shook. Not a little, but mightily and fearfullly; and so strongly that not only was its dense soil broken and split, but even the greatest rocks deep down were torn and rent.

Heaven and earth were united at the death of the only-begotten God, and truly worthily. For when the great king came from heaven for salvation and life, he did not move heaven nor did he shake the earth. But [he came] quietly and calmly and very peacefully, as the holy Spirit sang in the mouth of David: "He will descend like rain on a fleece"[30]. For when it rains on a fleece there are no noisy sounds or crashings or resounding quakes, but [it falls] very quietly with unheard and unseen sound. "And a fleece," says [scripture], not separating and cutting the fleece from the living [animal] and putting it aside — for that is the custom of men. But while it was on the animal **[p. 287]** the rain descended on it, cleaned away the dust, washed the stain, made the wool grow, made the animal lively. In such fashion the holy Spirit in the likeness of dew moved in the holy virgin with great power — an unheard, unseen [but] visible form. As it wished, so it completed what was worthy, peacefully without disturbance or movement.

[30] Ps. 71.6. For patristic interpretation of this theme see Lampe, s.v. *pokos*. Cf. Elishe, *On Joshua*, pp. 178-81. It does not appear in Ephrem's *Commentary*.

He came to this spot where it was right to effect this peace. But they did not wish it, but carried out the opposite upon him. Do you see that the same in return was requited upon them?

Because he is God, there exist no opponents to him, but from all sides totally appear supporters; as at the quaking of the rocks and the rending of the earth the tombs were opened, says [scripture], and many of the dead rose from their tombs and entered the holy city and appeared to many[31]. It does not mention the names of those arisen, nor does it show each one's house. Likewise it does not reveal the number of the risen, but only says "many." The "many" are not defined and distinguished by a numerical quantity, but from each other receive their abundance — like five with regard to three, or ten to five, but still more compared to ten. The limit of multitude is not bounded. If you reach the very end of numbering, there remain many more unnumbered than numbered. But because they truly arose, the veracious evangelist established in writing both the resurrection and the multitude. Just as he introduced the [word] "many," by the same word he also indicated the appearance was not to separate [persons][32]. They appeared to many, he said, without revealing the name of any one.

Every action appeared new and marvellous at the crucifixion of our Lord Jesus Christ, because the world was to be made new. And I shall say in brief that the same action which was worked there at the cross, not mine nor that of other men but the same Lord's, was predicted by the mouth of the holy prophets. "And that day, says [scripture], will be a great day, because there will be no light and no darkness, but [it will be] cold and clear. And that

[31] Mt. 27.52-53.

[32] Separate: *anoroš*, i.e. there were not separate individual appearances.

day is revealed to the Lord, [**p. 288**] because it will be neither day nor night; and in the evening it will be light"[33]. Do you see the revelation of the holy Spirit? From the beginning of creation such a day had not occurred, save only at the crucifixion of the Lord. For that day would not be light because the sun was hidden. Nor would it be dark, says [scripture], because the hour of evening had not yet arrived. Because at mid-day the sun set, he said "darkness" and not "evening." Because the warm rays were restrained, he said "cold" and not "hot;" and "cold" — not a little, but "clear," chilly, resembling winter which does not produce fruit. And winter indicates the hatred of the evil one which was done to the people. Furthermore he said: "In the evening there will be light." The hour of evening is neighbouring and close to dark night, just as this world was near to the final end and was neighbouring the endless darkness. In the evening of that great day the undarkened light shone out from the cross on the souls of those who were able to see the divinity of the Son of God and were illuminated with the same, so that darkness might no longer rule over them.

"And that day, he says, is revealed to the Lord." That revelation is not in one aspect or two but complete in all aspects. What greater revelation of the day than that, because everything became new and fearsome — the darkness new, and the night new, and the day new. New was also the rending of the curtain, new the quaking of the earth, new the splitting of the rocks, new the opening of the tombs, new the multitude of the resurrection of the dead, new the revelation of those who appeared to many, new also the holy city. Indeed I said that everything was new. For the cross was new, and new also the one crucified, and he was

[33] Zech. 14.7. See the *Teaching*, 474, for this quotation in a similar context. It does not appear in Ephrem's *Commentary*.

Renewer of all those renewed. Therefore [the evangelist] did not write down the names of those who arose nor of those to whom they appeared. For they were the likeness and example of the day of the great resurrection. They will not rise individually, nor as part of many, but all together without number or naming. By saying "new" many times, we are not at all missing[34] the newly-worked things which were all made new.

[p. 289] When the Jews saw, says [scripture], that Christ had lowered his head and released his soul, they begged Pilate because of the sabbath that they [the bodies] might not remain for the night on the cross, but they might break his legs and bring him down from the cross. The soldiers came and broke those of the robbers. But when they came to Jesus they saw that he had died, and they did not touch him. But one of the soldiers with a lance struck his ribs, and immediately there came forth blood and water[35].

Behold a new and wonderful sight! Who ever saw one of mankind that after his death his ribs were pierced on his corpse, and blood and water came forth? Before this it had not happened; and after this it will not happen, save only to the body of Jesus Christ. And this [did not occur] outside the prophecy, but through the soul of that same wounded one. "They will turn and see whom they wounded"[36]. Those who did not wound ask, but they do not see the one whom they wounded. Some wound, and others see and receive not the wounded one but the one who is healthy and heals wounds, and not only visible wounds but also invisible afflictions, and as medicine blood [for] blood and water [for] water[37]. If you wish, receive [this interpretation] truly. For

[34] Missing: *vripeal*, "failing to attain," perhaps here "omitting."

[35] Jn. 19.31-33, not a direct quotation. This is not in Ephrem's *Commentary*.

[36] Jn. 19.37 = Zech. 12.10.

[37] The last phrase is obscure.

water is the essence[38] of all living things, and blood [is the essence] of the life of all bodily things. With the blood is mingled a part of the effusion of warmth[39] and with the water is mixed the great power of the earth, and with both kinds are united all the elements, and they demonstrate the essence of the body of God the Word, which he took truly — the nature of our essence which he himself fashioned in his certain[40] creation.

So there came forth water for the washing of the holy font, and blood, the cup of the new covenant. For by water we cleanse ourselves of sin, and by the blood we become participants in the passion of his death on the cross. Unwillingly they fulfilled the scriptures regarding their own selves and for the advantage of the Gentiles: prophets of the truth, but not of their own will; labourers, yet they work the ground of another; merchants, but they accumulate wealth for another; leaders, yet for another they open **[p. 290]** the door of life; readers, but for another they expain the meaning of the testaments and the parables of the truth.

"They begged Pilate, says [scripture], that they [the bodies] might not remain for the night on the cross." Well did you disown the one who was removed from you and given to the Gentiles. Because death cannot be a neighbour to life, you too renounced at the evening hour the wood of life, so that you might hide under the shadow of the darkness you loved. In the same will be your habitation. Your unworthy requests which you begged of the judge — that they might break his legs and bring them down from the cross — for two thousand years and more you could not

[38] Essence: *goyac'ut'iwn*, as above.

[39] The author alludes to the common Armenian theme of the four elements, *tarr*: fire, water, air, earth, which are also interpreted as warm and cold, light and heavy.

[40] Certain: *anšušt*, "infallible." The meaning is unclear.

break the bone of the lamb according to Moses' command[41], yet the lamb of God you at the same time crucified and wish to break [his bones]. That which the holy Spirit does not permit for you, of your own volition you wish to carry out, which you cannot. But for what purpose then would the Lord do this? He gave himself to death to become a sharer in the torments of the word; he did not accept to have his bones broken, which I shall explain briefly.

According to nature and the moral[42] the essence of our bodies consists of two [aspects]. The softness of flesh and the parts of the active intestines [are] the matter of the female part, and it provides the cause of life through the nourishing of bodies. But the nerves, sinews, breath and bones [are] the power of the male essence. This is what is according to nature. But the moral [aspect] is the matter of the female part, of the entire corporeity and the abundance of nerves and bones with a certain masculine solidity. It resembles through its impassible solidity the unbreakable heavenly mind. Therefore the physical, the animal part of the lambs was given in Egypt as food for the people. But the bones with the other parts were preserved for the likeness of the rational aspect without being broken and crushed. Therefore the lambs were sacrificed as an offering to God and for burned offering, and not for a lack of fulness, but only for wisdom and for a mystery perfected in the future existence, as is indeed apparent in the sacrificing of the lamb of God. He gave his whole self through mankind, and handed over the whole man to God the Word. **[p. 291]** He fulfilled in himself all the previously written words of the prophets, and will perfect you all for God.

[41] Ex. 12.46. See p. 244 above for the exposition of the pascal lamb as an image of Christ.

[42] Moral: *baroyakan*, the Greek *ethikos*, used here as a neuter noun.

"They broke, says [scripture], the legs of the brigands. They came to Jesus and saw that he had died"[43]. This is a veracious saying and true image. For just as he was perfect in his divinity, likewise he was perfect in his sufferings, willingly and not unwillingly, because of this [saying]: "Lest his bone be broken"[44]. But the wounding in the ribs which he received [is] a source of outpouring for the world, renewal of the water of life, which will cultivate even more, not the trees of the garden in Eden, but the living trees[45] in the church of God.

[43] Died: *katareal*, which could also mean "been perfected;" cf. p. 283 above. The double meaning is immediately picked up in the following sentence. In Jn. 19.33 the text of Zohrab reads *meřeal*, "dead."

[44] Jn. 19.36.

[45] Trees: i.e. the just; see Lampe, s.v. *dendron*.

[*On the Burial*][1]

[p. 291] Then after the completion of all this, the burial of Jesus also received definite testimony from the race of the Jews. For all the witnesses of the death of the Son of God came together, but not all were united participants in his life. "Joseph came, says [scripture], a just man, noble according to nature and rich according to the world,"[2] secretly from men but openly to God. He not only was not found [participating] in their works of evil, but neither in their plans of impiety. So see the valour of the man. At the time in which everyone had united and abandoned God, he alone was armed in secret with weapons of virtue and took to himself the host of the army of faith. He was encouraged in himself, and before entering battle saw the victory — that "I shall fight together with God and overcome mankind." But I know that some on hearing this are not at all astonished on hearing these spoken words. And this is the habit of untested minds. Do not, brother, reckon this an abbreviation. For the place is awesome and the hour is fearful, and the fear of death is upon him who dared say that the man died in righteousness. Not only did the priests

[1] There is no heading in the text, but the editors so mark this section in the headers to pp. 291-299. A, p. 268, begins here with the same title.

[2] Mt. 27.57 "rich," Mk. 15.43 "a modest noble," Lk. 23.50 "a doer of good works and just." See Lyonnet, pp. 90-91 on this conflation; cf. Ephrem, *Commentary*, XXI, 20.

remove him from their prayers, but they put him to a death more cruel than that of brigands. Likewise the evangelist explains the man's virtue as not insignificant, but mighty and great.

[p. 292] "Joseph of Arimathea came; he was emboldened and entered to the judge and requested the body of Jesus"[3]. When you hear "he was emboldened," do not think it insignificant but a diligent effort in soul and body. In soul, because faith was greatly needed at that hour; for he did not remove as it were the body of a mere man, but as it were the body of the Son of God. Furthermore, in a bodily regard, not only did he have fear of death from the people, but more especially from the judge and his servants. For they thought: "What is the request of this man? [He requests] a man against whom such a multitude bore witness that he was guilty of death, who in accordance with the law of criminals was crucified and died. Yet this one requests him as faultless and innocent, put to death unjustly, the great and true witness of God. Perhaps soon on us too will fall punishment."

This man did not consider all this, but as he had previously been confirmed in the truth of Christ, even more did he remain firm at his death. Removing the body of Jesus, he wrapped it, not in haste or carelessly but with much thought and energy, in clean and honourable linen and with much myrrh and sweet-smelling incense[4]. This did not occur outside the foresight of the holy Spirit. Likewise the gold which he earlier received from the magi he represented through the image of the coin[5], saying to the sons of the people: "That on which the image of the emperor is found is appropriate to him; but that on which my image appears is mine"[6]. For men

[3] Mk. 15.43.
[4] Ephrem's *Commentary* does not include the anointing of the body.
[5] Coin: *dahekan*, as Mt. 22.19, Mk. 12.15, Lk. 20.24.
[6] A curious expansion of Mt. 22.21, Mk. 12.17, Lk. 20.25.

who are in authority set up statues in their own name, and they engrave their faces on the coinage, because through the engraved image of gold they are glorified and honoured in the world. I engraved my own living image on the living face of man. No one bears in the world the likeness of God, save only man. God appears to no one, save only to man. God loves no one from among [those on] earth, save only man. God alone loves man, and man alone loves God. God is man's and man God's. For man's sake God became man, and for God's sake man became divine. **[p. 293]** Therefore we went and gave Caesar's to Caesar, and God's to God.

This offering Christ previously received from the worship of the magi: gold, as I said, for the honour of kingship, but myrrh and incense for the death of the one wounded and buried. He was wrapped in linen by the hands of men, that you might be clothed in the garments of the glory of the Son of God. The corpse of his body was anointed with myrrh — which is the duration of immutable time from long past — that he might anoint you with myrrh for the duration, not in time but for the immortality of the renewal of the holy Spirit. He was embalmed with incense like a dead body, he who is to embalm everyone for a sweet odour, which emanates from the light of life. He was placed in a new tomb in which nothing at all had been placed. So instead of your tomb I shall lead you to the heavenly city which will be formed without the work of hands.

"So he put a great stone as cover at the door of the tomb and departed"[7]. You do well, O lord Joseph, for you become a true witness of the burial of your Lord. For you know the ingratitude of your race, that perhaps tomorrow they will deny that "we ever put him in that tomb." For there are many who are false, and you

[7] Mt. 27.60; cf. Lk. 23.53.

also are many who do not know how to lie. Nicodemus, your co-worker, he it is who entered most skilfully with the Lord into an examination of the sayings. For the diggers of the tomb bear witness for you, the merchants of the linen also bear witness, the hundred pounds[8] of myrrh bear witness; those who lay out the corpse also bear witness, those who anointed the Lord's body. The hands of the helpers bear witness, who propped up the stone at the door of the tomb, that it would be right to call it a tomb and not resurrection of life.

O my lord Joseph, I have remembered also your great witness the judge, to whom you went and requested authority to remove the body. Now why did you do this? If all would be united with them in falsehood, when you too will have the risen one in [your] midst, what will they have to say? If they obstinately persist against you, **[p. 294]** as they are indeed accustomed, you will tell them how you gave him in bonds to Pilate, and Pilate gave him to the soldiers, and the soldiers delivered him to the cross, and the cross delivered him to the tomb. So you will have the choice, either give me the dead one from the tomb, or take, receive the one arisen. But if you do not choose one of these, you have nothing else save to depart and go away from this risen one, which indeed you did. So do you, my lord Joseph, rejoice and be glad. For the first Joseph was great, truly worthy of the greatest revelations. From Joseph greatness was extended to Joseph. The former was witness to his unspotted birth from the holy virgin; and the latter was witness to the burial of the same[9]. And from these two true witnesses will appear another multitude of witnesses of his luminous resurrection.

[8] Jn. 19.39. Pound: *litr*, as Zohrab.

[9] Ephrem, *Commentary*, XXI, 20, stresses the parallel between the two Josephs; cf. Lyonnet, p. 93.

"Then the priests came to Pilate. Lord, they said, we remembered that that errant one said that after three days I shall rise from the dead. So command that they guard his tomb, lest perchance there be some trick from his disciples and many go astray after the report. You have been given, he said, a band of soldiers. Go and keep watch, as you know [best]. Receiving this command from the judge, they sealed the tomb"[10] with rings on the two sides. O cautious priests, you did well because you took care. You who could not guard your own selves, wish to be guards for another. And you who went astray from the road, call him errant and deceiver. Whence do you know that he is errant, and is not rather worthy to show everyone the true path? Perhaps you will mock the magi who deceived Herod, because there was no advantage to set him on the true road?

"We remembered, they said, that errant one." It seems to me that you give your response confusedly. It is not right for you to call him errant, but the one who misleads you perverse ones. As [scripture] said: "They went astray in the desert[11] and not on the road." For what purpose then it would be said by the holy Spirit, the inspired narrative indeed makes clear: "He did not lead them through Palestine along the shortest way, but they went around in the desert[12] for forty years"[13]. **[p. 295]** So that all their transgression might be expended in the desert, and then having been punished they might be worthy to enter that land of gifts. As I think, you went astray not in a desert but in a city, not from the land of promises but from the Lord of heaven and earth. So coming to the judge you call him "errant." He who led astray is called true?

[10] Mt. 27.62-66.
[11] Ps. 106.4.
[12] Ex. 13.17-18.
[13] Ex. 16.35, etc.

If he is errant, permit it. It is not necessary to doubt his words. But if what he did earlier is true, you cannot deny it. Likewise, if you still [deny], they are many more than you who bear witness to his working miracles: not only living persons cured of pains, but those who have departed in death and returned thence through resurrection; not only the sons of your nation, but also many of the Gentiles and even more of the demons. So if all these do not call him "errant" but the one who brings back those gone astray, then if to you only he seems errant, go and keep watch; perhaps you will be deluded, and then you will seek further reasons confusedly later on. Behold the judge appeared beneficent to you. He carried out everything you said, your evil wishes. And now not one man or two gives you help, but a whole company of soldiers, and the company not of equals but under a leader and chief who was important and loyal to the judge.

They went in all readiness and with their rings sealed the doors of the tomb in order[14]. They themselves stopped there with great care, watching without sleep lest some trick be played. Oh wise ones, or rather, very foolish ones. If he wishes to rise from the dead, then he is able to do everything. He did not open the doors of the tomb, and did not break the seal, and did not show himself to you. How will you be able to know that he whom you placed inside the tomb will rise? You are very thick-headed[15] and even more sluggish in intelligence. He reckoned that those soldiers of the judge would be uninformed like outsiders and not insiders. You who saw such great miracles, even at the hour of his death, were still stupified and you did not **[p. 296]** understand how you could guard the one who moved the earth and shook the heavens

[14] In order: *dasu*, i.e. in order of rank.

[15] Lit. "thick-hearted."

unless you were guarded by him. For I cannot blame the soldiers, since they are servants of the judge and they are compelled to carry out his commands. But the priests and interpreters[16] deserve much weeping and tears. They leaned stone on stone and enclosed the rock within — or rather the Creator of heaven and earth. And they placed their rings on it, and the guards kept watch.

Do you see their foolishness? You cannot be guardian of your own thoughts. While you stand in this holy place, you are found in an unworthy place. You are in the city, and you see Italy[17]. You work on dry land, yet you sit on a ship at sea. You are on earth, and above the heaven of heavens you move around with troops of angels. But I know about you that you were never able to rise up from this earth and see the companies of heaven; but continually dragging yourself along the ground here you resembled your equal[18], your father. For not only did you feed on earth, but you were choked by the earth in soul and body. Therefore you do not know what you do. For just as you were in everything ashamed in front of the judge and all the host of the people, even more will you be ashamed in front of the soldiers who guard the tomb. When they tell you the truth, you will fall into agitation of doubt. You cannot make them out as false, because they are reliable. You do not wish to reveal and justify [their story], because you are blinded in your eyes from the judge and the people and also from God. So what will you do? Alas and woe to you! There

[16] Interpreters, as above at p. 247, for the scribes. Here the Pharisees of Jn. 27.62 are intended.

[17] Italy: *Italia*, i.e. an impossible distance from Jerusalem. The earliest Armenian texts refer to Italy as "Dalmatia," e.g. Aa 874, *Teaching*, 689. Here the verb is singular, but plural below.

[18] Equal: *andravar*, one of a pair of horses.

is no consolation and no place of refuge, save only with that same one whom you slew and buried. And because he is kind to men, he receives you and does not remember the earlier transgressions. But I know that you will not do this, because you are not worthy. But you will run to the temple, because you still have thoughts of false hope. I know that you will enter into a plan and your mind will run to cursed silver. You will lose your silver, and with it your own selves and all those who will listen to your error.

[p. 297] Now our Lord Jesus Christ carried out all his saving work with regard to those under the sun, and set off for the lower region of the earth in all his power in order to descend and see the power of death, and to give consolation to the descendants of Adam, who were sitting hopelessly in darkness and in the shadows of death[19]. When he arrived at the strong wall of hell and at the iron gate with bars of bronze, the fearsome voice of the great Precursor[20] made the wall totally shake and collapse. The power of the living fire melted and destroyed the strongly-barred gates like wax. The rays of the self-produced[21] light spread out everywhere and penetrated to the inaccessible hollows and niches of its remote places. The solid darkness was consumed and dissipated, and the infamous ugly form of the ruler of the underworld[22] was nakedly revealed.

[19] For Christ in hell see also Elishe, *On Joshua*, pp. 190, 196, *On Baptism*, p. 211, where both Christ and John the Baptist preach in hell. The Harowing of Hell is a popular theme in Armenian, based on the *Gospel of Nicodemus*. See, for example, the two texts translated by S. Der Nersessian, "The Armenian Version," and "A Homily," in both of which the master of hell is distinguished from Satan.

[20] Precursor: *karapet*, a title associated in Armenian with John the Baptist [though not used in the gospels], but in Heb. 6.20 applied to Christ who "entered within the veil." See the previous note for John in hell.

[21] Self-produced: *ink'nacag*, as p. 279 above.

[22] Ruler of the underworld: *sandarametakan*, as in Phil.2.10 of "those under the earth," and p. 299 below. But here the adjectival ending *-akan* is used in the sense of "lord of, commander of." For the term *sandaramet*, see Russell, *Zoroastrianism*, 324-329.

Then death screamed, raised a clamour and wept bitterly. He called out loudly, saying: "Who is this who has come and entered into my impenetrable stronghold, who has stripped me of the natural darkness which is my garment? I burn from the fearful heat of his fiery glory. There has not remained for me a nook of darkness of gloom of night, nor plain for escape or mountain for hiding, no valley for refuge. There is no distant place whither I may flee, or any chasm nearby that I may occupy. The depths shout out that he is here, and the mountains melt like wax before his glory[23]. He has taken all Tartaros captive; he has toppled the forces of darkness, my sinister soldiers[24]. Woe to me, O wretched me! He has robbed my treasures, he has plundered all my riches. He did not leave me any hope of consolation, nor a single one of my own supporters.

Who then may he be, because I do not know? Enoch and Elia did not come here. Abraham and Isaac and Jacob did not do this to me. Noah and Abel and all the just have fallen under my control. Moses and all the prophets are subject to me. Melchisedek and all the just kings did not rebel against me. Why should I number individually by name the generations of men and women? Behold from the beginning until today the righteous **[p. 298]** and the sinners, the powerful and the weak, the old and the young, even those who did not see the light of the world, have gathered in my presence. All stand subject to my authority. But who may this one be, let someone inform [me]. If I were able to know whence [he came], perhaps I could think up some expedient. If he is from earth, then I would know the province and family. The nature which I see bears the likeness of human progeny in

[23] The mountains... glory: Ps. 106.5.
[24] Sinister: *jaxoy*, "of the left hand."

every respect. Especially I find that the number of parts of his body is not more or less, but his are as those of all. But by his face I am greatly terrified. For if in his descent to me he plucked away many from me, woe to me if he comes here with evil intention. I fear that he will take absolutely all [of them] with him, and I alone shall remain of all my people.

I also have great dread of his person, because not only does he deprive me of something, but he does not even leave me my dark place. As I understand it, from this darkness he will send me to another darkness. How I wish that that darkness where he was intending to take me was like this one. But if it were suchlike where he would lead me, then he would not drag me hence. Now behold, it has become clear. Just as I did not know his province, likewise I do not know the darkness to which he will take me. But this is the worst evil of all for me, as it seems, because not only has he come here for the sake of the just but also for all the sinners. If he makes a reckoning with me and demands from me the bones of the dead who came to me, perhaps I can give them up. But if he requests Enoch and Elia from me, and if he makes this further [reckoning] with me, then I have a most serious danger and worrisome perplexity, for I find nowhere to go."

Now when death was agitated in himself with all this and could not find from anyone a word of consolation, then hell[25] responded to death and said: "We know that one's nature and we recognize his family. It is he about whom the holy Spirit previously spoke: "Princes, raise up your gates, and may the gates of eternity be lifted up, and may the king of glory enter"[26]. If you repeat twice or thrice and ask many times, **[p. 299]** you will hear the same:

[25] Hell: *dzoxk'*, not *sandarametakan* as above.

[26] Ps. 23.7-9.

"The lord of powers, he is the king of glory." When death heard the name "lord" and "powerful" and "warrior" and "coming to battle with the authority of death," all his power dissolved and faded and broke, and hope for his kingdom was dashed. Stricken with fear of his face, he made urgent haste to flee and hide, but found no place. Raising his voice in great entreaty, he said: "I know you Jesus of Nazareth. You are the holy one of God. Do not torment us before [due] time"[27]. Now when he had bound him and nailed him with nails, he nailed his feet and his hands, and he tightened and bound them through the power of the invincible cross, and he gave power to all men who believe in the crucified one and carry out the command of God the Word to tread on serpents and scorpions[28] and on all the power of death. He took much plunder, and brought it away and distributed it to all believers.

While the Lord was performing all these heroic acts, the guards were asleep and the priests were eating the bitter [herbs] and the unleavened bread[29]. Now the Lord earlier than the time he had appointed arose and appeared to the angels. But he did not disturb the tomb, nor did he open the door, nor did he break the seals, nor did the guards become aware of him. The angels were exceedingly thankful at this, because in previous time they had not been able to look on or see the hidden glory of the Son of God. But today he came for the sake of our salvation, and carried out in order all his dispensation for those above and those below and those underground[30]; and there appeared a new fruit for a

[27] A conflation of Mt. 8.29, Mk. 1.24, Lk. 4.34, 8.26.

[28] Cf. Lk. 10.19, but here the text follows Ps. 90.13.

[29] Ex. 12.8, and parallels.

[30] Those underground: *sandarametakanac'*. Here the adjectival ending has a different sense from the use at p. 297 above.

new world in new fashion — new and primeval. First the angels received it and rejoiced at its sight, which previously they lacked. Because the angels had desire without envy and a holy love without falsehood, they made great haste to give the good news to the women, not only in words but also by visible sight. Immediately they rolled away the stone from the door of the tomb, and entering within worshipped the place where God made man had lain for the salvation of sinners and the life of the departed. **[p. 300]** They bowed down and kissed the rock, and greatly honoured the Lord's [resting-]place, and wondered in amazement that the one for whom the heaven of heavens was inadequate as habitation in his love for mankind had restrained the greatness of his glory, had descended and lain in this little spot, where he had reckoned it sufficient to be for three days.

Then straightway they fulfilled the saying which David had spoken: "Let us worship at the place where his feet have stood,"[31] and again: "Worship the foot-stool of his feet, because it is holy"[32]. So dear was the place that not only did the angels enter inside, they also sat down, says the evangelist, one at the head and one at the feet[33]. Now when you hear "they sat down" do not immediately go out of the place; for not indeed did they sit in a temporal [sense]. But they sat and sit and will sit, until that day on which there will be union of us and of the angels and of that world to which Christ went for three days, and appointed a time for all to gather at the door of the same tomb[34].

[31] Ps. 131.7.
[32] Ps. 98.5.
[33] Jn. 20.12.
[34] A, p. 278, ends here with a doxology.

[*On the Resurrection of Christ*][1]

[p. 300] So I greatly love that spot, and I do not wish to distance myself from the door of the tomb but to sit there with the angels, and see the great miracles, and hear from the mouth of the same angels who were speaking with the women and proclaiming the word of their good news throughout all the world. For those women are entitled to the name "mothers of the Lord;"[2] and by faith they are recognised as great and wonderful. For they know the same Lord as without mother in heaven and without father on earth; and in the compassion of the great love they had for him they brought sweet oils to pour over the tomb.

Because sleep had been removed from their eyes for those three days and three nights, very early Mary Magdalene came to the tomb[3]. Since the angels had rolled away the stone, she looked inside, but did not see there the Lord's body. Therefore she wept in great mourning and said: "What shall I do, whither shall I go, where shall I seek? They brought him down from the cross, [p. 301] placed him in this tomb, sealed the doors with a stone,

[1] There is no title here in the Armenian text, but the editors so mark this section in the headers to the printed edition. A, p. 279, begins here with the same title.

[2] Mothers of the Lord: *teaṙnamayrk'*; this is the only use of the plural noted in the *NBHL*.

[3] Mt. 28.1, Mk. 16.1, Lk. 24.10, Jn. 20.1; cf. Ephrem, *Commentary*, XXI, 22.

and guarded it carefully. I bear witness to his disciples that nowhere was there any movement all this night. None of the Jews did this because of respect for the great sabbath. There was no interest among the Gentiles. It is not allowed for any person to go around as a corpse-stealer. There is no suspicion of animals because of the weight of the great stone, and especially because of the watch kept by the soldiers. If I suppose a resurrection, this is very early. On the evening of Friday he was buried. Behold, that is two nights. But today is one full day and two hours; and he said that for three days and three nights he would be in the heart of the earth[4]. How could he who spoke the truth in everything, in this respect have lied? God forbid! I cannot doubt him. He never spoke falsehood but the truth in everything. For everything that he said during his life did occur and was fulfilled. So would he lie in this only? But I do not know if he has indeed arisen, or whether he has been stolen away by someone."

This she said, and beat her breast and shed tears. She dared not cry out loudly for fear of the priests and caution with regard to the soldiers. But in her heart she grieved, and in her mind she choked, and she found no consolation for her situation. Eventually the angel in his great compassion took pity on her and said: "O woman, why do you weep in despair, and make mourning inconsolably? Tell me the reason for this; perhaps you will hear a truthful answer." She said: "Because they removed my Lord from the tomb and I do not know where they put him." The angel said to her: "You have a beautiful love for the holy faith; but not wisely do you shed your bitter tears over this tomb. Who ever heard or saw that the dead seek the living, or that men are in

[4] Day, full day: Elishe here distinguishes *tiw* [day], for the daylight period of twelve hours, and *awr* [full day] for the period of twenty-four hours.

search of the living God? It seems to me that you are more foolish than the guards. So if you wish, come approach this spot and see that he has arisen. He is not here. And why indeed do you seek the living among the dead?" Saying this he cast the woman into great doubt.

[p. 302] Once more the angel spoke to her: "Although you do not believe me as a stranger[5], ask your compatriots who are friends of the judge and familiar with your priests. They will tell not only you who are friends but also his enemies. But the time of his resurrection even I do not know. At the shaking of the earth, then I thought that he had risen. At the tomb were many of my companions and myself, but none of us realised. We all looked at the door of the tomb: the stone remained unmoved, and the seal was clear. But we had our suspicions from the earthquake. We opened the door and did not find him inside. Eventually, he himself took pity and appeared to us for a while. But now we too do not know where he is. We cannot leave this spot, however, since he loves so much the stone and the cross and the tomb hollowed in the rock, and especially you who are seeking him. Because of all this he will again have compassion on us, and we shall once more become worthy to see the one risen from the dead."

While the angel was saying all this with the woman, behold some of the guards were bestirred and entered the city to tell the high-priests. "O, why do you stay, they said, why do you sit down? See what you have done. He has truly risen; we are unable to hide it. Behold we cry out at the palace of the judge, and to all the city we raise a clamour. We cannot deny the awesome sight of the resurrection, because this last earthquake was greater than the first; for we happened to be present at the time of the crucifixion

[5] Stranger: *awtarašxarhac'i*, "one who inhabits a foreign land."

and we saw the miracles and terrors which occurred. But for us that day was easier than this day, because from the earthquake not only were our hearts striken, but also some men appeared to us. We do not know from whence they were, from earth or heaven. They were exceedingly luminous and awesome, and so bright that if they appeared at mid-day the rays of the sun would be eclipsed through their inacessible light. But we are astonished how you did not see, or how the heat of their fire was not felt here. The stones of the place boiled, and the earth dried up. [**p. 303**] We fell down half-dead; and many of us who remained there are still dead."

When the high-priests heard all this from the mouth of the soldiers, they began to respond: "When such fearsome deeds have been done so that you say that some of you had fallen down half-dead, how were you able to come and tell us?" The soldiers replied and said: "Some blessed women came to the tomb while it was still night; they were bringing sweet oils and wonderful incense like divine gifts. As the women approached the tomb it was a great relief for us at that time. Blessed be those women, and blessed the city whence they were. Truly we bless such women. We were thus benumbed and lying down unable to rise, when one of them fearlessly and without hesitation approached the tomb and looked in. When she saw that the body was not there, she burst into tears and wept bitterly. Concerning the dead one she heard from the men that he had risen and was alive. She then realised that they were angels and not men, who very familiarly indicated to the women concerning the crucified one [that they should] confess him as God and not man, as alive and not dead. For since we had been relieved at the coming of the women, we ourselves indeed heard from the mouth of those who appeared, as they said: Why do you seek the living one among the dead? Do you not remember what he said earlier, that it is necessary for the Son of man to die and be buried and rise on the third day? If you do not remember that, then look: He has risen; he is not here; and he precedes you to Galilee. There you will see him. Behold I have told you"[6].

When the high-priests heard this, they were greatly astonished and their hearts were broken. They realised that they were not reporting on some pretext. They took counsel and said: "What then shall we do, since he arose so clearly and men and angels saw it? The guards whom we requested from the judge describe the risen one with great signs. Now he is going to Galilee, and will work great miracles there."

[p. 304] Since they were not able to think of another expedient, they laid hands on the treasures of the temple. They gave much silver to the guards, and instructed them about the reasons for the first order, concerning which the soldiers had been commanded by the judge.

Now Mary, surrounded by the angels, embraced the tomb and sought the risen one. In her very warm love she ceaselessly cast her eyes around the spot until the desired sight was granted her — not of some angels but of the Lord Jesus himself. For the evangelist writes: "When the angel had spoken to her, she looked in the direction of the place where they had crucified Jesus, and she saw there the Lord, but was unable to recognise him and thought he was the gardener. She said to him with supplicating words: Sir, if you have removed him, tell me where you have put him so that I may take him"[7].

Well did you keep watch all night, O Mary, and beautiful is your search of the morning. No one among mankind deprives his hired workers, nor does God deny the wages of your labours. The

[6] Lk. 24.5-7.

[7] An expansion of Jn. 20. 14-15.

angel pays you the wages of your night's work, by giving news of the one risen from the dead; and the appearance of the gardener puts to flight the ardour of your heart's desire. As it seems to me, you have found the thief, and not only the thief but with the thief the booty. Grasp him well; it is truly he, not another's stolen property but his own real self. Did you not say "you removed," as if of something belonging to another; but he is indeed himself. This is the one who was placed in the tomb; this is the one who rose from there; this is he who was crucified; this is he who went to the dead; this is he who entered the house of the powerful one; this is he who bound that strong one; this is he who plundered his treasures; this is he who distributed gifts to many; this is the true gardener; this is the one who brought the brigand into paradise. Him you were seeking; for him you were weeping; about him you heard from the angel that he had risen; for him you lamented; for his sake the angel moved around the tomb; for him you brought oil and incense. If for him you brought them, do not seek another.

But as for what you said: "Where did you put him? Show me, so that I may take him and go," **[p. 305]** I know that you said it out of your love. And if he gives himself to you, you cannot take him away, nor can the other Mary of the family of James, nor the Mary of Cleopas, nor the sister of Lazarus, nor the Virgin Mary who is his mother. Even if you are all united you cannot remove him, because he became heavy. He is consequently onerous[8] for those who wish to approach him bodily, but light for those who approach him by faith[9] — which now you will hear from him.

[8] Heavy, onerous: Elishe is using the stem *canr*, "heavy, difficult," in the two senses.

[9] A, p. 284, ends here with a doxology. This 1836 edition does not contain the other homilies translated here: *On the Appearance to the Disciples*, *On the Appearance at the Lake of Tiberias*, *On the Preaching of the Apostles*.

For when Mary recognised that it was Jesus, says [scripture], she addressed him in her old custom, saying "rabbuni," which translated means "teacher"[10]. Behold Mary, you are in the body and bodily you weep; bodily you speak, and bodily you search. Now just as he had compassion and revealed [himself] to you in the same previous form, likewise you wish to approach him physically[11]. Therefore you will hear the response: "Do not approach me, because I have not yet ascended to my Father"[12]. Why then did he say this? Because he was the fruit of the new tree of life, he did not accept that women should approach him before men. He thought it sufficient to honour the gender of women through their giving birth. But he makes the revelation of the resurrection through the angels, who have affinity with the male gender[13]. By the intermediary of sight and through the leadership of the angels he appeared to the women, and sent [them] to the disciples.

He indicates two things in this place. He teaches Mary about his own elevated nature by naming his Father in heaven; and he consoles his disciples by calling them brothers. For when he says: "I am going to my Father and to your Father,"[14] he makes himself equal to the disciples, and he indicates that his Father and theirs is one. He mentions his own individually, but that of them all together. There is a great separation and division between them, and he is understood by revelation in the souls of the wise. Because he is man according to the nature of all, he makes himself equal with the world. He is God uncreatedly with the Father;

[10] Jn. 20. 16.

[11] Physically: *t'anjrut'eamb*, from *t'anjr*, "dense, solid." See the Introduction for this term as used for the Incarnation.

[12] Jn. 20.17a.

[13] Gender: here *azg* for women, *bnut'iwn* for men. In Greek *aggelos* is masculine, but Armenian has no grammatical gender, *seṙ* [as Dionysius Thrax, p.13].

[14] Jn. 20.17b.

he separates himself not only from the disciples but from all rational existence. "To my God, **[p. 306]** he says, and to your God." Behold we know that he is our God, creator and king and lord. And if we thank him for his creative power, he is our king, overseer, and guardian. And if we do things opposed to [him], he is our lord; he judges, punishes, and leads [us] to the right path.

That he is your Father, Lord, we know because we have learned that truly from you. How do you say: "I go to my God and to your God?" Yes, he says, because he is your Father by creation, and he is my Father by birth. He is your God, as I said, according to creation[15], and he is my God according to dispensation[16]. But mine, he says, individually alone; whereas yours, not individually but totally, of mankind and angels and heaven and earth and the elements of existent things[17]. Just as the Father in his benevolence, without anyone asking, through his Son created this world, all things visible and invisible, with the same philanthropy his Son also, at the will of the Father, took upon himself the body of our nature and accepted sufferings in his own body, even to the death of the cross, to burial and resurrection. For that reason God became flesh[18], and consequently no longer body but God. And God not without body, and body no longer heavy by nature[19], but a divine body, without quality, without number, without time, without place. God the Word is indivisible and indissoluble, always ineffable and indescribable, and with him the body also is ineffable. Always God himself in himself, not in a place but the

[15] Here *hastołut'iwn*, "fashioning," not the usual *ararč'ut'iwn*, as just above.

[16] Dispensation: *tnawrēnut'iwn*, a calque on the Greek *oikonomia*.

[17] Existent things: the plural of *goyac'ut'iwn*, for which see the Introduction.

[18] Became flesh: *marmnac'eal*. There is no distinction in the Armenian *marmin* between "body" and "flesh," the Greek *soma* and *sarx*.

[19] Heavy: *canr*, as above at p. 305.

place of all; not in time, but time [derives] from him; not in creation, but things came into being through him; far superior to everything, heaven and earth, and the nature that surrounds the heaven of heavens. With him understand also the body born of a virgin. Because of all this we have the right[20] to be called Christ's brother, and with that also [the right] to call God father to us; because with the one part which was united with God the Word, which rose up, entered heaven, and sat at the right hand of the Father, all parts of our human nature received the gospel of hope. For by him and through him we shall be raised up and attain and inherit **[p. 307]** that place which is without passion or torments, where the Son of God sits on the right hand of God.

Therefore the Lord sent Mary Magdalene to the disciples, saying: "I am going to my Father and to your Father, and my God and your God." Mary went and told Peter and John that she had seen the Lord and that he had said this to her[21]. When Peter heard this, he was reminded of the previous saying of the Lord: "After three days I shall rise up"[22]. He immediately stood up with John and they both ran to the tomb. Because their haste was so great they vied with each other. John arrived first; he took a look but did not enter inside. When Peter arrived, they both together entered and saw that the tomb was empty and devoid of the great treasure which had been deposited there, save for the linens because these had fallen and were lying on the raised rock. But the napkin with which they had bound his head was not lying mingled with the other linen, but had been folded up separately[23].

[20] Right: *išxanut'iwn*, as Jn. 1.12.

[21] Jn. 20.17-18; Peter and John from 20.2, where Peter and "the other disciple whom Jesus loved" are mentioned, but the latter is not named.

[22] Mt. 17.23, 20.19, 27.63, Mk. 8.31.

[23] Jn. 20.3-7. Ephrem's *Commentary* does not include vv. 2-5.

Now what does this indicate — the falling of the linen, and the napkin not mingled with the linen? It is clear to all according to natural science[24]. The heavenly inhabitants have no need of earthly clothing. Now the Lord of heaven and earth in his self-existent hypostasis[25] and natural glory was born from the holy virgin. So did he not ascend to the Father in that same hypostasis in which he came to us from the Father? But I shall speak according to our natural [condition]. So then, the Lord of this world came into the world for our sake. But when he took our [characteristics] into his own, there was no need of ours. He left the linen here, and through the linen remaining behind the world remained as if in mourning and in torment through this sight, so that you yourself might adorn it according to your teacher. For you were completely naked in the world; and while you were in the world you were raised according to its need. But when you will go hence, you will not be able to take anything with you. As you came, so will you go. If you understand this in advance, the mode of your life will resemble that of the angels; and the path of your leaving[26] will follow the Lord.

[p. 308] But with regard to the napkin we see a great mystery. For the resurrection was of man and of God: of man according to nature, of God according to non-nature[27]. The two being united, they no longer appeared as two but as one existent being. Very

[24] Natural science: *bnaxawsut'iwn*, a calque on the Greek *physiologia*.

[25] Hypostasis: *zawrut'iwn*, perhaps here "power;" see the Introduction.

[26] Leaving: lit. "end, death [*katarac*]."

[27] Non-nature: *tarabnut'iwn*; see also p. 312. This abstract noun is not attested as such in the *NBHL*. The adjective from which it is derived, *tarabun*, is used in two senses: "that which is different from nature," or "living in a foreign land." In the latter case it is equivalent to *tarabnak*, which is a calque on the Greek *apodemos*. But "departure," or "death," *apodemia*, does not seem appropriate here.

paradeigmatic appeared these things at that spot, which the great apostle indicates to us with reliable testimony: "Her husband is the head of the woman, and Christ is the head of the man, and God the head of Christ"[28]. He ranked the world [from] head to head, and he led all to the Father of all. Therefore the napkin appeared as the most honourable among the other linen, so that you might truly understand no distinctive separation and no solid unity[29]. The head is not of someone else, but of him whose is the body. And the body is not another's, but of the same head. The body is not the head, nor is the head again feet. But the many limbs are ordered and established and arranged according to each body. Because honour is to the head, with the same head all the parts of the body also were honoured.

Now if such is the view among us, how much more so for the spiritual nature. The Godhead is head, the Sonhood is head, the holy Spirit is head. Come, with the eyes of your mind look and see, and hear with faith the saying of the Lord: "No one knows the Father except the Son, and [no one knows] the son except the Father"[30]. Through the holy Spirit are recognised Father and Son with that same holy Spirit. For God is Spirit and Spirit God; Spirit Son, Spirit also the holy Ghost. Now because this is so, the Father is not Son, nor the Son Father, nor the holy Spirit Father or Son. The Father [is] creative power, which is an example of the royal power. The Son [is] natural power, whereby is revealed the legal[31] power. The Spirit [is] conciliating power, whereby is clearly revealed the life-giving power. It is called consubstantial deity[32].

[28] I Cor. 11.3.
[29] This passage is unclear.
[30] Mt. 11.27.
[31] Legal: *datołakan*, lit. "judging."
[32] Consubstantial: *miasnakan*, common in the *Teaching*; see p. 253 above.

The Son is content with the natural name, which is power and wisdom, and birth itself and uncreatedness. The holy Spirit is pleased in his own self and in existence **[p. 309]** by derivation[33] from God, ineffable and indescribable. The will of God resided[34] in the divinity of the Fatherhood, which is the cause of things speakable and things ineffable. So he rolled up and placed the napkin to one side. Christ himself honoured his own head. So who is greater, who then would pay honour, save the one who will be honoured? If another received honour from someone else, such would be the case. But if he himself honoured himself, how will you be able to show divisions in the indivisible? Just as between Christ and his own head there is no separation to be introduced, nor between Christ and his Father, but there is a single mystery of honour so that he may teach the twelve...[35]. The Father raised, the Son arose, the holy Spirit proclaimed the news to creatures. Just as in creation there was equality — so the beginning of existence for this new world was the resurrection of Christ. Therefore the holy Trinity was there complete and total, and at the same time all the powers of created things.

Do you see that there was no need to take the linen with him? Instead of the linen he put on[36] the whole world and adorned the world with the Father's glory. He revealed the mystery of the tomb and the linen and the napkin to the head of the disciples. For the tomb is the likeness of this world in which we are buried; and the

[33] Derivation: *hanołut'iwn*, not attested in the *NBHL*. The stem can render the Greek *exago*. See Lampe for the use of this verb in the sense of "bring forth, produce," regarding God and the Trinity.

[34] Resided: *hanguc'eal*, lit. "rested."

[35] The editors do not indicate the length of a gap in the Armenian text shown by 11 dots.

[36] Put on: *zgec'aw*, very common in Armenian for the Incarnation; see the Introduction.

temporal linens are the winding-sheets of its attractions. But the honour of the napkin, as we said above, is the hopeful expectation of those who with open-looking eye are able to see from afar the Father of all, who will honour the head of all those who become worthy of the crown of heavenly gifts.

But perhaps one of those who are desirous of learning[37] wishes to enquire and hear [the answer to] this also. Who rolled up the napkin for the head and placed it to the side — the Lord himself or the angels? Let such a questioner know that everyone carries out the providence of God, rational [creatures] and irrational. The rational ones carry out his commands through their senses, **[p. 310]** but the irrational elements through their natural movements. Now the angels are superior in rationality, and by their habitation are closest to the divinity, knowing the mystery of his will. As it appears, for love of their Lord they were moved to great affection for the tomb, and entering inside they expressed their emotions on the linen, lifting them up and putting them down and often kissing them, like someone who finds the object of his desire, grasps it in his embrace, and is greatly excited; and what it is right to do, I do not know. In this fashion the angels acted with the linen. Picking up the napkin, they folded it and put it to the side, in the human fashion of chamberlains who work in the palace and put all the king's garments in a respected place. But to the crown they pay separate attention, and do not keep it mixed with the other clothes. In this same way the heavenly hosts of our heavenly king descended to serve, shining light around the desirable tomb. Two entered it, honouring the whole of the place. But

[37] Desirous of learning: *usumnasēr*, used of monks by Elishe, *On the Transfiguration*, p. 232. But the word is too widely applied for any precise group to be identified here.

they did not mix the crown with the rest. By placing it separately they taught mankind the consubstantial sovereignty of the Trinity, whence we all received our existence.

[*The Appearance of the Lord to the Disciples*][1]

[**p. 310**] Then Peter, understanding this mystery, went from the tomb amazed in his mind. He entered the house with the other disciples. Because there was great trepidation for fear of the Jews, with great care they kept the door locked, sitting in silence. Many agitated thoughts entered their hearts, and they reckoned themselves like orphans and unprotected. Persecuted by the Jews, abandoned by God, and long since estranged from their families, they appeared at that time the most sad and mournful and pitiable of men. For there was no one among them who could open his mouth or speak to them a word of consolation.

While they were in this tribulation, Jesus came, stood in their midst, and said: "Greetings to you"[2]. This was great amazement and an awesome vision. The doors were locked; [**p. 311**] around the building extreme caution was observed; there was no entrance within at all. When the Lord saw that their hearts were still in a state of shock, he immediately showed his hands and side, so that from the great and obvious signs they might recognize the Lord, and he might drive out the depression of their hearts. He [spoke] a second time and encouraged them with a second greeting.

[1] There is no title in the text, but the editors so mark this section in the headers to the following pages.

[2] Jn. 20.19.

Because confusion and peace are opposites, he proffered the greeting of helpful peace. He expelled and cast out from their hearts their confused perturbation, and dispelled from them earthly mourning and sadness. He rendered them firm in mind and undisturbed in spirit.

When from all sides he had cleansed them of earthly contaminations, he strengthened and toughened their souls more than the hardness of adamant, so that they might be able to receive his ineffable grace, which is greater than and superior to all, and with which nothing of things visible can be compared. How shall I weigh [something] against that, which is invisible and inscrutable and which is the life of all things visible and comprehensible? What is that, so much grander and superior to everything; I cannot tell. I understand that "he is,"[3] knowing truly that God exists. He is believable to me; his nature[4] I do not know. I merely know that which is visible; the invisible [properties] of God, God alone knows. But behold I have been forced to say what I do not know. For just as he entered through locked doors, and the walls remained intact and the doors were not broken down, and he in his total self was inside and even showed his hands and side to them, and twice strengthened them with a vocal greeting — in the same manner the Lord grants to his disciples those gifts, he whom the sea cannot contain nor the dry land support nor do the heavens suffice for his habitation.

So say what you must say. For how long do you magnify the immeasurable? Behold I wish to speak, but I soon renounced knowing. Furthermore I am greatly afraid. Perchance when I shall speak you will not bear to listen. And in your not enduring it, I

[3] He is: *ē*, as Ex. 3.14.

[4] Nature: *orpisut'iwn*, or "quality."

hesitate whether you may indeed die; and that you may die not only according to nature, [**p. 312**] but both according to nature and according to non-nature[5]. But I know that you here oppose me and say: "Whence did you hear that; and when you heard it, why did you not die on the spot, but you live up to now and expect to continue living?" Yes, that is so. Not only to now, or a little more, do I expect to live; but I have become immortal. "If indeed this is so, tell me that I too shall hear and receive and become immortal."

I say that you will receive. But be purified, cleansed, and made totally pure; fully cure yourself of, and throw off, earthly passions through tortures and torments. Prepare yourself for the heaven-bound elect. Set yourself apart from all cares of the world and all its abominations and deceitful amusements, which are the splendour of this temporal [existence]. When I abandon all this, what will he give me for all this? I shall tell you. Only believe, only hope, only will, only take pleasure [in this], only grasp and follow. Where shall I go and whom follow? The crucified one. And where will he lead me? Home. Whose home? Where the disciples sit gathered, and the doors are locked. Through what he wishes he enters, and creatures do not prevent him. And if you wish, you can. His nature, he says[6], leads him. Believe, take confidence, and you can enter with him. He humbled heaven and descended in his coming to you. Believe in his first coming and you will fly up in your ascent. He was born of the holy virgin, and her virginity was not impaired. You have faith in the virgin-born God the Word, and you are born of the holy virgin of the font, and are called brother of Christ; and the virginity of the font is not spoiled.

[5] Non-nature: *tarabnut'iwn*; cf. p. 308 above.
[6] The subject of *asē* here is not clear.

He received in his own body the sufferings, and through [his] passible body he removed the sufferings of all bodies, and he was preserved unharmed from all evil. Believe also in the holy sufferings of Christ, and share his sufferings in your passible body, and preserve your soul unharmed from all harmful passions of the world. He, because he was not guilty of death, died, and was buried, and rose from the dead, and did not open the doors of the tomb. Believe in the one buried and risen, **[p. 313]** who comes to destroy all tombs, and to raise up all those sleeping without imperfection or lack. So if you put on his power of faith, and enter the house of Peter, and sit with all the disciples with the same faith, you will receive the same greeting. And through that same greeting you will again become worthy of that great gift which I am about to describe.

For when the Lord stood amidst the disciples in the house he had entered despite the locked doors, that house resembled heaven and earth, and all the adornment and angels of heaven, and all living beings, and mankind on earth, and especially the Father himself and Son and holy Spirit. Just as at the creation the statement: "Let us make according to our image," is understood in accordance with the number [of the Trinity][7], but "he created" according to the image of God, and "he breathed spiritual [breath],"[8] according to the single hypostasis — so also in this house twice [there was] a greeting. "As my Father sent me, so I send you,"[9] is understood according to the first triple number. But that he breathed on them and said: "Receive the holy Spirit in yourselves, and if you forgive anyone their sins, he will be forgiven; and if you

[7] For this exegesis in Armenian of Gen. 1.26 see the *Teaching*, 275.

[8] Gen. 2.7; but Elishe has *imanali*, "spiritual," for the *kendan*i, "living," of the Armenian biblical text.

[9] Jn. 20.21.

bind anyone, he will be bound,"[10] this again leads back to the first [statement?] at the beginning of the account, recapitulating: "God made everything; and God saw everything that he had made, and behold it was very good"[11].

Did you come then around the house, as if yet another needed to come? Behold you indeed came and entered within, and in few words told everything. But you were unable to convince them all. Why then? Because not all were inside. And if the house was heaven, who remained outside? Often I question the sayings, and another makes response[12]. He who did not have faith, he was outside. For without faith it is impossible to receive the holy Spirit. Behold this is the great gift which I was unable to express, and yet I was forced to speak. If anyone is presumptuous, and wishes to approach the power of the Spirit without faith — if he is a priest, like Caiaphas, he is rent and split; **[p. 314]** and if a layman, like Anania and Sap'ira. So who would be able without great help to receive the creative holy Spirit, unless the Lord himself were to breathe [on him], saying: "Receive the holy Spirit in yourselves"[13].

I am astonished at this and very amazed, how the walls of the house remained firm and the floors were not broken. But then I remembered that the house was the heaven of heavens. As if the king were to dwell in a desert, that desert was "built up,"[14] and consequently they call it a great city and not a desert. More than that, this house became a heavenly city, and those inside heavenly citizens, and those who were not there are still earthly ones through the difficulty to persuade them. But if the same Lord

[10] Jn. 20.22-23.

[11] Gen. 1.31.

[12] The sense of "another," *ayl*, is not clear.

[13] Jn. 20.22.

[14] Built up: *šinec'aw*. The stem means basically "inhabited," hence "settlement," or "building," and by extention "prosperity."

himself were to be present with the same power, one would receive the same grace. So one would be able to share the lot of the twelve, and especially if the same Lord were in the same house and place. If you wish, listen to the evangelist, for he told everything truthfully: "Thomas, he says, one of the twelve, was not with the disciples when Jesus came and appeared to them"[15]. For although he heard from the others, he did not at all agree to believe them. But he wished to be an eyewitness and to examine very closely the wounds of the nails. If you remember what I told you previously[16], how very difficult it is for aquatic [animals] to live on dry land and for terrestrial ones in water, it is even more difficult to accept the gifts of the holy Spirit without faith, just as this disbelieving man disputed in argument, opposing his companions.

O my lord Thomas, is not faith derived from listening? If you see and examine and comprehend what is true, it is no longer called faith, but truth. From the Lord you have often heard of his suffering, dying, and resurrection. The disciples through the symbol of words spoke with you and related to you the manner of his revelation. That they are not false, you well know; and that the Lord spoke rightly, of that you are informed. Why are you so firmly stubborn? If I do not see, you say, I do not believe. Behold you see indeed. Will someone perhaps not censure you? No, he says. Let him only appear to me, **[p. 315]** let me merely see. For if I see and examine, then I shall render my own mind free of scruples. And if someone blames me, I shall accept it; I shall not be ashamed by such a one. I know the sweetness of my Lord, that he is benevolent and merciful. I am not greater than Peter, he says,

15 Jn. 20.24.
16 There is no clear parallel in the preceding homilies.

nor is my lack of faith [worse] than his great denial. And if his tears were for him salvation, then for me my shame will be forgiveness. But only let me see him whom I long for. If I am able to say this too, I shall beg the Lord that he appear in the same house with the same revelation, not only with doors locked, but also with the same greeting in the midst of the same household. Behold I have declared my wish. I am not able to issue a command, but I wish to make a request. If I am worthy, may he help my weakness.

Now the one benevolent to all, when he saw the ardour of the disciple's affection, had mercy and pity on the perturbation of his mind. But he permitted that the days of the number of the first signing[17] be completely fulfilled before the circumcision of his lack of faith be circumcised, and then he might be worthy to be renewed and receive the gospel without hesitation, just like his fellow-disciples. For the evangelist shows: "It was, he says, after eight days the apostles were again there in the same spot inside the same house, and Thomas was with them. Jesus entered among them, the doors being locked, and said: Greeting to you. And to Thomas he said: Put your fingers in my hands, and your hands in my side. See and verify; and do not lack faith, but believe"[18].

When he had said this, Thomas was overcome by shame and fear together: he was ashamed by his companions and frightened by the Lord. He said: "My Lord and my God." Why first "Lord" and then "God"? It was not thus at the creation. During the five days the name of the "Lord" is not mentioned; the name "God" is introduced and does everything. But on the sixth, then the name of the Lord appears[19]. As is apparent, the cause of these matters [is

[17] I.e. the eight days [before circumcision, Lk. 1.59, 2.21].

[18] Cf. Jn. 20.26-27.

[19] I.e. Lord, *tēr*, appears for the first time in ch. 2 of Genesis. For the importance of the number six see p. 254.

as follows]. Since the name God is a creative power, it is also propitious [**p. 316**] and benign and creative. But where there is creative activity, there is no longer a legislative [activity]. Now if creatures were to come to judgment, there is need of a legislator, just as this apostle made clear. By discerning wisdom he responded and said: "My Lord and my God. For I have fallen, he said, under the judgment of my lack of faith. Judge me, because I am worthy of punishment. But do not expel me from the number of your disciples. I know that my transgressions are great. Many are the witnesses of your resurrection. And it is necessary for me to believe not only the multitude, but also your very words with which you constantly taught and instructed us, and which by deed you accomplished. So since you have mercifully appeared in this spot in your previous manner, and you have displayed the unbelief of my thoughts, and the eyes of my mind have been opened, and face to face I have seen my Lord — I shall be able to say: "My Lord and my God." For by your reproving me you have made me a new man, and you have not left in my soul or in my body occasion for judgment. Consequently you are my God. And as you are my God, thereby you are also Lord, thereby also king, thereby also Father, begetter and fosterer, giver of gifts and of the inheritance of everlasting life."

But perhaps someone may say: "Behold three times the Lord appeared in the same house. Why did he breathe on Peter and his companions and say: "Receive the holy Spirit on you," yet did not do this to Thomas? For if the fulfilment of the bestowing grace is the holy Spirit, it appears that this apostle lacked it." I shall say concerning this as much as is necessary, not new or discordant, but what you all know and have received by faith. The holy Spirit of God is the creative power, and pours out the mercy of his love on creatures. But he himself is understood as inseparable and indivisible. But the grace is not from himself but from him[20]; the gift is not from himself but [he is] the bestower of all. Just as his own Father is from himself in essence, likewise the holy Spirit is in accordance with Father and Son. Now when the Son said to the disciples: "Greeting be with you," **[p. 317]** they were all filled with the holy Spirit. But because he breathed on them, he recalled the first creative activity[21] in this second one, namely that he who made the first man, the same is also he who came and saved and renewed. Now in saying: "Receive the holy Spirit in yourselves," there is a contemplative meaning[22]. Just as the Son put on the body of our nature by the will of the Father, the holy Spirit had the same wish. For just as the Son put on humanity, likewise our humanity put on the holy Spirit, so that through the holy Spirit we might put on the Sonship and Fatherhood[23]. If it were not truly thus, how would we be able to call God a Father to us, and Christ a brother to us, and the holy Spirit a renewal for us? Since we are bone from the bones of Christ, and also mind from the mind of the Father, likewise too the power of the holy Spirit.

But again if anyone were to ask: If you said an indivisible and unmingled power of the holy Trinity[24], I am not denied by my own words, nor do I oppose yours, nor do I compare the Creator with creatures, nor do I destroy the immoveable nature. For the Godhead is immutable, but our [nature] has fallen subject to many corruptions and changes, and it needs the help of the creative power. For he who created, the same will renew to incorruption.

[20] From him: *i nmanē,* referring to the Father [?].
[21] I.e. the breathing of life at Gen. 2.7.
[22] Contemplative: *tesakan,* the Greek *theoretikos.*
[23] Put on: the verb *zgenul*; see the Introduction for such vocabulary.
[24] Power: *zawrut'iwn,* or "hypostasis." See the Introduction for this term.

As we have often said: He gave the holy Spirit as renewal through breathing on the disciples, and through the same Spirit he will renew all creatures, and especially the nature of our humanity. He divided [it] into many parts, and one Spirit is necessary for binding and linking them all, just as one may learn truly in one's own body.

So I beg you. Look around yourself at yourself and see the mixture of your nature. The body is one, yet the limbs are many. And each of the limbs in their division is without malice or envy and mutually friendly, and they all work [together]. When they receive compensation according to each one's labour, none of them reckons the gift its own individually; especially if there is achievement **[p. 318]** in running by foot, or strength of hand, or rhetorical skill of discourse, or wealth of mind in wisdom, or indeed whatever part of the body it may be. For they do not run confusedly, but they are arranged in order according to the set number of parts of the body[25]. So then tell me: which of them will receive the gift? I know, you have recourse to the head, yet the feet are not envious. And if the hands receive it, the others are not irritated. If only there is honour in the body, then the joy is common. Likewise the name which man has is imposed[26] and not natural, since that is not sharing in the great achievement. Before the body the name is attested and honoured and crowned. The parts of the body have wounds and scars, yet the name inherits the valour. The limbs all rejoice happily with the name, and thus there is unity to the whole multitude. So if it appears thus with regard to one man, how much the more through the Son of God, who put on the one

[25] Elishe does not give a number. Išox, pp. 88-89, numbers the bones, veins, sinews, etc.; cf. Abusaid, p. 118.

[26] Imposed: *drakan*, also rendered just above as "set" for the number of parts.

body in accordance with the numerically single man, and as one man possesses all humanity.

So if he breathed on them and said: "Receive the holy Spirit on yourselves," those who are inside [the house] are numbered. But we do not know if they all received the holy Spirit. Thus one should not fall into perplexity of doubt here. For it was not the place which purified the persons and made them worthy to receive the Spirit, but the Lord of the place, since the place appears holy because of the Lord, the Lord is in every place. While he was in heaven, he was on earth; and while he was on earth, [he was] in heaven; and while he was in the house, he was in the world and in every place and with each person and [all] mankind. So he was with Thomas, and thus with all.

Did he breathe on the believers? Yes. But not on any of the unbelievers, although they were inside the house. Hear the same Lord when he speaks to Thomas, not praising him but blaming him: "Because you saw me, you also believed. Blessed is he who has not seen, yet believes in me"[27]. Would you then consider this blessedness as something small? **[p. 319]** If a man reckons a man blessed, that would still be a great thing, let alone if God blesses a man. For if, when the man who has not seen him believes, he reckons him blessed, what do you think this blessedness is save the holy Spirit?

If again you were to say: "Behold Peter and his companions were believers, as you say, and had received the holy Spirit — what need was there of a second breathing?" You question like a man, and like a man you are ignorant. The invisible things of God you do not know; but to him even our secrets are clear. Likewise again for you what is necessary is not breathing, but first

[27] Jn. 20.29.

faith; and through faith you can then receive the holy breath, not by the mouth and not through the nostrils, but by the spiritual sense of God. How do you know who were in the house and how many they were? I did not speak in vain. And of what had they need? Did I not say that they were times of great disturbance and everyone was in turmoil? Although they were confirmed in faith, yet it was necessary to offer consolation to the believers. And the only consoler is the holy Spirit[28].

Now as for my saying: "Who were there and how many were they?" I did not say it pointlessly. For the cause of disturbance was no one else save sin; and power of sin is Satan; and the power of Satan, demons. Now by the Lord's breathing on the apostles, saying: "Receive the holy Spirit on yourselves," demons were expelled, Satan retreated, sin was destroyed, the apostles were filled with the holy Spirit. By saying: "Receive on yourselves," [he means] I do not force it [on you], because the divine Spirit does not enter into a doubtful person, and does not dwell in a deceitful soul — but in holy bodies and in pure souls and in believing minds. "Receive, he says, on yourselves by your own will, and carry out the will of the holy Spirit."

When you hear "he breathed" pay attention, examine a little, be critical in your mind rather than in your eyes. For he did not say anyone's name, and he did not breathe individually on everyone, but "on them, says [scripture], he breathed." And by saying "on them," according to the scripture it appears that [it means] those who were in the house; but according to the spiritual [meaning] **[p. 320]** on the whole world. And by saying "on the whole world," it appears that [it means] on every man. And by saying "on every man," [it means] through the true faith. For

[28] As Jn. 14.16, etc.

where there is faith, there is also God; and where God is, everyone is there.

Now when the apostle heard from Peter and his companions: "We have seen the Lord, and he spoke such and such with us," and he by faith had accepted the report of the vision, then that same revelation occurred to him, the same greeting was with him, the same breathing was on him, the same holy Spirit appeared to him, as the Lord himself said: "Blessed are those who have not seen, yet will believe in me"[29]. As we said above, if there is one body of a single man, and many parts, and unity overall, then this world also is one matter, the creation of one hand, yet divided into many forms. And the types of forms, according to each one's kind, equally and in unison all look to the one whence they have their existence and life, [namely] God. The chief and leader of all is man, superior to all by natural intelligence and acquired virtues. The summation of them both is belief in the Son of God[30].

Now in whom is found true faith, in him are seen all who are without passions and sufferings, as the great Moses had inspiration from the holy Spirit. And from the same grace of the Spirit which Moses possessed by the providence of God, the seventy-two elders were filled[31], and they prophesied among the people. Yet Moses was not deprived of the grace of the holy Spirit. Although some were envious, he was even more filled with the holy Spirit and desired that all the people of the Lord turn to prophecy. So it is the same Lord who bestowed on Moses the holy Spirit, and in the house breathed the same Spirit. For through a small number

[29] Jn. 20.29.

[30] I.e. faith is the summation [*katarac*, "perfection"] of intelligence and virtue combined.

[31] But in Num. 11.16 there are seventy. For the fluctuation in Armenian exegesis between 70 and 72 see the *Teaching*, esp. 503.

innumerable multitudes will believe in Christ, they will receive the same grace of the Spirit without rancour or envy. For the gift is not a part but all parts of the divinely-given grace, whereby he created heaven and earth and all existent things that are in them. **[p. 321]** But perhaps one should thoroughly investigate the number of the twelve on whom he breathed the holy Spirit, although not all of them. But those who love very willingly the wisdom of souls and bodies will attain the ranks[32] of the twelve apostles, who are four threesomes, and six twos; and summed up together they become twelve. The beginning of the unit is the breathing of the holy Spirit on the head of the twelve[33]. And from the one and the two and the four is fulfilled and completed the number seven, so that in the six may be seen the creation of the world, and in the unit one the completion of the seven, and in the four the material elements. Now in one six the number three is completed by three doubled, and it bears the likeness of the uncreated, self-existent power without beginning. The one is a superior name to the three and ineffable, solely spiritual, which is indivisible. From three the triple number is rendered complete. Furthermore, according to the seven is also seen the existence of our senses, which are divided into seven parts of forms: eyes and nostrils, and ears and mouth[34]. At the beginning of coming into being through the same number the world was created by its cause, which has the likeness of the one, in six days in which the species of beings were brought into existence. But by progressive increase in the one, which is the seven, added with the number six, it increases and multiplies and is completed as the number

[32] Ranks: *vičak* means both "rank" and "lot, fortune."

[33] For Peter as "head," *glux*, cf. Eznik, 384. In the *Teaching*, 467, he is called "first," *ařaǰin*.

[34] See p. 280 above for a different interpretation of the seven senses.

twelve[35], in which all things are seen, heavenly and earthly: heavenly — the sun and moon, the five planets and seven fixed stars, which make two sevens. And from these two sevens take their being all created things subject to passion, which are the causes of life and the duration of this world. Furthermore, by that same number seven the heavens possess seven spheres, which are called "belts"[36]. They are levels of air separated from each other by an open interval, a circular formation by the command of the Creator, the causes not only of existence below the sun, but also of life and living well, and contemplative understanding for heavenly wisdom.

This the prophet Isaiah described, filled with the Spirit of the Lord, and he saw **[p. 322]** that all creatures are very great and wonderful[37], and in it [the world] is understood its creator and establisher[38]. And he heard further from the same Spirit speaking in the mouth of David: "Since your works are great, Lord, and you created everything with wisdom"[39]. Truly are they great, because God is seen in his works; and they have been made with wisdom because they were created through Christ, and Christ is the power of God and the wisdom of God. Just as it was [created] through the wisdom of God, which is Christ, likewise also through the holy Spirit, as the same David said: "Through the Spirit of his mouth are all their powers"[40]. By saying "his" [he

[35] The syntax and meaning of this part of the sentence elude me.

[36] Sphere, belt: *parunak*, *gawti*; see Thomson, "Cosmology of Vardan," for these ideas.

[37] This is closer to Ps. 135.4 than to any passage in the Armenian text of Isaiah.

[38] Establisher: *hastatič'*, only in Ps. 17.2. The form *hastič'* is found in Is. 22.11 and elsewhere.

[39] Ps. 103.24.

[40] Ps. 32.6.

means] of the Father through the Spirit, but "their" [means] of creation. Now where he says: "The heavens narrate the glory of God,"[41] he reveals the divinity. But where: "You created everything with wisdom," there he refers to the Son of God. But where he mentions "mouth" and "Spirit" and "power," there [he refers to] the holy Spirit co-existent with the Father and Son.

Isaiah through the grace of the holy Trinity, in accordance with the seven spheres of heaven divides into seven parts the giving of the same Spirit. Grasping heaven and earth he brings them to a single unity, saying as follows: "A rod will come forth from the root of Jesse, and a flower will come from the root, and the Spirit of God will settle on it, a spirit of wisdom and intelligence, a spirit of counsel and power, a spirit of knowledge and piety; and the spirit of the fear of God will fill it"[42].

So by often mentioning the number seven, which is that of the supernal nature, the prophet Isaiah summed up and came back full circle to the Word of God, who created heaven and earth at the beginning. He gave his form and typified himself in the creatures; and coming to his own, accepts his own, puts on his own. And he put on, not by chance[43] and not by some accident, but he gave himself form through heaven and earth and what is in between: through heaven according to the one, which is God the Word; and through earth, which is our earthy existence[44]; and through the middle, through the numbered zones in accordance with the seven senses. Just as he took our earthly body, which is a part of the earth, likewise too [he took] the airy and **[p. 323]** fiery

41 Ps. 18.2.

42 The seven gifts of the spirit: Is. 11.1-2, 1 Cor. 12.28.

43 By chance: *dipuacov*, lit. "by contingency."

44 Earthy existence: *hołełinut'iwn*, an abstract noun derived from the adjective "earthy."

which are from heaven and are in us through Christ. The Lord possessed the same in his own body, in which everything is fulfilled. For through him is the beginning of coming into being, and the fulfilment of the renewal of the new world. Because the senses which are in us are a much finer nature than the denseness of the body, they have a relation to the spiritual intelligence which the prophet called parts of the soul. And truly [so], because with our ears we heed God, and with our eyes we see the creatures in which God is understood, and with our nostrils we absorb the breath of air which is the life of all, and with our vocal organ we render praise to God on behalf of the creatures.

Now if that is the case with us, what are we to understand with regard to the Lord's senses? He stands on earth, and with his eyes sees the Father in heaven. He moves about in Galilee, and the smell of Lazarus's death is noticeable to him from afar. The interpreter[45] in his mind blasphemed in his soul, saying: "If he were a prophet, he would know who and what sort of woman approaches him"[46]. But the Lord heard [that] like a very loud clamour, and reproved him with parables of the two debtors in words appropriate to our likeness. Without ears all elements heed him, the water in the pots[47], the loaf in the hand[48], the winds at sea[49], sins in mankind, the dead in the tombs[50].

Now this is what the prophet Isaiah said: "There will come and settle on him seven spirits,"[51] through the seven senses which

[45] Interpreter: *meknič'*, as above for "scribe," p. 247, and Pharisee, p. 296, as here.

[46] Lk. 7.39. But the printed text of Elishe reads *oč'*, "not," for *ov*, "who" [sic!].

[47] Jn.2.7.

[48] Jn. 6.9, with many parallels.

[49] Mt. 8.27, with many parallels.

[50] Jn. 11.38, with many parallels.

[51] But the text of Is. 11.2 reads "the spirit of God" for "seven spirits," though seven qualities are then enumerated.

the Lord assumed and [by which] he worked all the accomplishments of the holy Spirit, and in himself completed the heavenly seven and the earthly seven, which is the first beginning and the final completion. For we begin from the unit, which is the foundation and establishment; and we come to completion in the seven, which is the summit and conclusion — not of the numerical part but of theoretical wisdom. For in six, says [scripture], God made everything, and on the seventh he rested[52]. Does God rest? Never. How could I say that he rests, he who does not labour? But consider well and reflect. What is the resting of God, save that his will is accomplished? Whoever of created [humanity] **[p. 324]** was able to be pleasing to God and gave rest to his judging power, save the Only-begotten from the Father and the Virgin-born from earth, through whom God created everything and who came and worked everything pleasing to God? So then, this is the seventh day on which we say God rested, because in six days all things subject to passion were created, and God is far from passions and sufferings. He named [them] "good,"[53] but not passions; for it is possible for [one] of those subject to passion to become good, but not without suffering and asceticism. Where there is virtue, there much mortification of the body can be seen; and where there is mortification of the body, there days and months and years and periods of time have fallen under corruption. Therefore on the one day only there was holy rest, which is called sabbath, and by number seven. And the number seven adduces the likeness of the unbegotten, and the unbegotten that of the uncreated, and the uncreated possesses the creative power.

[52] Gen. 2.2.

[53] Gen. ch. 1 refers to God "seeing" that they were good; the verb "to name" is not used.

Now in the six days is seen a thousand years, in which the whole world had fallen under corruption, until the number of the seven arrived, which [scripture] named above "sabbath," and reckoned as rest. This is the coming of the Lord, who entered despite locked doors, and purified and cleansed the dross of the six first days. Through the name of the seven he granted to the twelve apostles that power which is virgin and unbegotten from mortal existence, and very productive without passions and sufferings, whereby they might put this world in order and set it aright from the six [ages] to the seventh age[54]; that they might be very productive for righteousness, and unbegotten from evil and hatred and all corrupting passions of this world — just as the very number twelve of the apostles has meaning[55] through the chief one, whereby they removed passion from the world, according to the twelve parts which were seen by revelation in the illness of the [woman] with flux for twelve years[56]. The woman had that individual pain personally, but the world was secretly tormented in the twelve parts of the day and night. For the day has the number of twelve hours, **[p. 325]** and equally so the night. And in an hour one day according to the number of days of a month[57]. And the whole day with its nightly parts was subject to emptiness. I say emptiness of beneficence; he who is devoid of the good is full of worthlessness. I call worthlessness the deprivation of truth, and deprivation is the abandoning of God.

[54] For the theme of six ages followed by one of rest see p. 254 above.

[55] Meaning: *tesut'iwn*, the Greek *theoria*.

[56] Mt. 9.20, Mk. 5.25, Lk. 8.43.

[57] The sense of this phrase I fail to grasp, since the twelve Armenian months had each 30 days. Perhaps Elishe is trying to say that one hour has twice thirty [minutes].

Because from the beginning men followed the enemy, and willingly entered into subjection to all corruption, [that was] the first abandoning of God. The second was to worship hand-made objects. The third, to sacrifice to insensible objects. The fourth, to be indifferent to corruption. The fifth, to kill one's fellow-image. The sixth, avarice, which is the root of cruelty. The seventh, hatred, which is the unfruitfulness of the just part. The eighth, theft, which is the beginning of the ruin of the world. The ninth, rapine, which stirs up wars. The tenth, falsehood, which is the rejection of God. The eleventh, pride, which is the ruin of souls and bodies. The twelfth, the fruit of death which we inherited in corruption.

Now with these twelve parts all the world had fallen into the affliction of illness, and there welled from it the blood of invisible wounds. Very often it had recourse to doctors, not because they healed, no indeed; they rather added severe wounds to the [original] wounds. Not only did blood flow from bodies, but also from invisible and bloodless souls, which was the outpouring of invisible corruption. For on looking up to heaven they saw the stars and went astray, [supposing them] to be the cause of this temporal life. They exchanged the timeless God for them here on earth in accordance with the twelve numbers, which the poets mythologised[58], saying as follows: There was some great one, they say and with him an immense time. When they approached each other, they begat six sons, whom they nicknamed Titans, and equally with them females whom they called Titanis. And they established offspring, and men brought passions for themselves from earth to

[58] *Aṙaspelabanel* is used frequently by M.X. to describe the singing of old oral tales, which he supposed were elaborations of originally historical events. For Titans see M.X., I, 6-14. The female *Titani* do not appear in early Armenian texts.

heaven. **[p. 326]** Gathering up great blasphemies, they launched them at the deity.

Through these twelve they immersed in blood the simplicity of souls like solid bodies in the two parts, souls and bodies. Not only did they sacrifice, but they were sacrificed. And we say were sacrificed: eyes, by looking lasciviously; ears, by listening to lewd sounds; nostrils, in smoke [sacrifices] and incense; and taste through insatiableness according to animal nature, whence dissolute desire multiplied. They all were immersed in the blood of the foulness of their deeds. Because of us the day was befouled, and in the day the twelve hours; and the year, and in the year twelve months; and behold at the same time also all this earth.

If through these earthly ones the earth was befouled, and through the heavenly, heaven, then when the Lord healed the woman who had a flux for twelve years, who was a sign of the pains of this world, it was indeed necessary to heal the world also. For the Lord did not come to the world for the sake of a part only, but for the sake of all parts of the world. He healed the one part, so that through the one part all parts might learn to run to the same doctor and to grasp, not the same hem[59] but the holy Spirit and they might see the holy Spirit in the twelve apostles. For the woman did not gain health by seizing the garment, but before [grasping] the clothes she grasped the faith. And by acquiring faith she became worthy not only to be saved from pains but also to see the divinity of the Son. When someone saw God, then he was united to him[60]. Just as the Lord himself does not only praise the woman, but also greatly wonders: "Who, said he, approached me? And much power, he said, went from me"[61]. When you hear

[59] Mt. 9.20, Lk. 8.44.
[60] This sentence is obscure.
[61] Lk. 8.45-46.

"approached" understand union with God; and by "much power went from me" [understand] the holy Spirit to be guardian and defender of the woman's faith.

Now if one man was thus filled with the immeasurable grandeur of God, how much more the twelve who received the breath of the divine Spirit and were filled completely, and filled the whole world with incorruption[62] through the same Spirit. **[p. 327]** Not only did they cure mankind, but also the day, and in the day the twelve hours and the year, and in the year the twelve months. How could the day be healed? I shall explain. Just as it was diseased, so was it healed. It was diseased in idolatry, it was healed in piety. In accordance with the twelve hours of the day men had gone astray after the twelve stars, whence the astrologers[63] deceived and deluded them. But now in accordance with the twelve hours of the day the voices of the prophets sound in the church, and the words of the twelve apostles are expounded, and they distribute the gospel of life to all believers. Thereby men are encouraged to virtue; and instead of their previous error they speak the truth and work righteousness and produce divine fruit: marriage in purity, virginity, mercy, kindness to strangers[64], hope in God, true faith, love without hesitation. And instead of the foul sacrifices which shed the blood of animals by offering them to demons, today the martyrs, willingly and not by force, shed their own blood for the blood of Christ.

These are the twelve apostles who purified and [still] purify the whole world. For the day is the beginning of time, and it

[62] With incorruption: lit. "without corruption." This seems to point to a Syriac text behind the Armenian here, being a misrendering of Syriac *d'la*.

[63] Astrologers: *astełagētk'*; for other attacks on astrology see references to texts in Thomson, "Let Now the Astrologers Stand Up."

[64] As Heb. 13.2, where also purity of marriage.

increased and was completed and reached the sixth age. When the days were purified, as we said, by the preaching of the apostles, the months and years and times and eternities were purified. For if the beginning is holy, then all who take increase from it were purified. For the number of the twelve apostles did not by chance attain the order of apostleship, but from distant times revelations appeared by God's providence. The first twelve [was the number] of the sons of Jacob[65], by which number his nation increased and multiplied and inherited the promised land. Again through Joshua there was a small revelation of the number of twelve stones[66], especially because some went up and some came down, like a clear wondrous vision[67], those ascending as from darkness to light, and those descending from light to darkness. **[p. 328]** Now the Gentiles who were submerged in the acts of their sins, ascended from the depths of the sea of sin[68] through the twelve apostles, who are the stones of truth. And winds and torrents are not able to move them, nor the violence of rains. Now the twelve heads of the people[69] came to an end and stopped. They descended and remained on the bottom of the river under the heavy water, and there they have been placed until today[70].

Likewise if we go to the desert in Galilee where the Lord filled the need of the people with the miracle of the multiplication of bread, while the remnants were not more or less but filled twelve

[65] Gen. 35.22.

[66] Josh. 4.3.

[67] Elishe turns to Jacob's ladder, influenced by the stone for his pillow, Gen. 28.11. Joshua's stones were carried from the Jordan.

[68] Sea of sin: see also p.333; cf. *Teaching*, 568, and the *Physiologus*, 36, regarding the kingfisher.

[69] Heads of the people: *azgapet*, as of the leaders of the 12 tribes at Deut. 33.21.

[70] Cf. p.333, where aquatic creatures are sinful.

baskets[71] — is not this view of the miracle obvious? Before the bread was multiplied, they carried the baskets empty, and they were filled from the remnants of the meal. Most worthily. For it was God who provided. He sated them for the present, and for the future heaped up wisdom. According to the outward[72] description it was the baskets that were filled with bread; but according to the hidden meaning, the twelve apostles were filled with the grace of our Lord Jesus Christ, and were scattered and spread in the twelve regions of the world. They filled the four sides of the earth in which all the nations of the Gentiles dwelt[73].

We have come often around the house, as we said before[74], which became earth and heaven, and became capable of holding all. It seems to me that we have been too involved with[75] the number twelve. For although we were not able to advance [our discussion] according to its merits, yet when the Lord himself will scatter and spread them [the apostles] through all nations by the power of the holy Spirit, then will be accomplished the word of the prophet who said: "I related and spoke, and they became more than number;"[76] that is, the churches of believers in Christ Jesus our Lord, to whom be glory and power, now and for ever[77].

[71] Only Jn. 6.13 specifically names Galilee; cf. Mt. 14.20, Mk. 6.43, 8.19, Lk. 9.17.

[72] Outward: *yaytni*, lit. "clear." For the contrast between the open and hidden senses of scripture see also p. 342-3, and Elishe, *On the Transfiguration*, p. 217.

[73] Elishe uses the same term *kołm* for both the twelve and the four, rendered here as "regions," then "sides." It is not clear if he means that the Gentiles, *het'anosk'*, the Greek *ethne*, inhabited only four of the regions visited by the twelve apostles. For the four sides see also p. 338 below.

[74] See p. 313 above.

[75] Involved with: *patec'ak'*, from the verb meaning "to surround, enclose." Perhaps there is a mistake here for *patmec'ak'*, from the verb "to relate" [as in the quotation following], i.e. "We have spoken too much about..."

[76] Ps. 39.6, referring to God's works.

[77] This is the only doxology in the text before the final paragraph.

[*The Appearance of the Lord at the Lake of Tiberias*][1]

Once more Jesus revealed himself to his disciples at the lake of Tiberias. For Peter and Thomas and [**p. 329**] Nathaniel, James and John the brother of James, and two further disciples were in one place[2]. So what does he do for them? He removed them from the house; he filled them with the grace of the holy Spirit; he sent them into the world so that they might do work. Without worries they were going around at leisure, and they were going about nowhere else save around the lake. They were unable to abandon their patrimonial trade, but were occupied in it, studious about it, engaged in it, and they wished to remember what they had forgotten. Do you see how great is the steadfastness of their minds? They were not dismayed, they had been so much advised and disciplined by the Lord, and informed by and imbued with the holy Spirit; yet they were not yet acute and so it was necessary to sharpen them further.

What do you say, my lord Peter? You sit at the lakeshore and you worry about the sea and you prepare your boat. "Let us go, you say, let us catch fish." Do you see that by saying that you urge to the same the other apostles, and they must follow you? For

[1] There is no title in the Armenian text, but the editors so mark this section in the headers.

[2] Jn. 21.2.

where the mind wills, there the feet lead. And the mind is the head, and you are the head of the disciples[3]. When you say: "Let us go and catch fish," what do you hear from them, save that they say to you: "We are with you." And because where they go you are their house and city and whatever may be necessary for your heavenly lot, do not forget[4]. Your number is beautiful. Behold you are seven. In you is seen the world, and at the same time also the Lord of the world. Yet your idleness is not good. If you are occupied with a refuge for yourselves and you have no other work, then go to Judaea, walk around the site of the resurrection, circle the rock, look around for the cross. Apply yourself, see where the priests hid it[5]. Examine the site. There will soon[6] be a search for the cross. The Lord does not leave in the earth his weapon with which he slew his enemy and removed the captives from him. Look carefully around the place; come by the doors; perhaps the angels will be there, as indeed they are. Go to Sion, mount to the upper room, look at the closed doors through which the Lord entered. Remember the spot where he came into your midst and greeted you, **[p. 330]** where he also breathed the holy Spirit on you. Apply yourselves to all this, think on the same, lest the great miracles which are performed among you be forgotten from your hearts.

But if you are afraid to go to Judaea because Annas and Caiaphas and all the cruel people are there, no matter. I do not blame you for that. The great James is there, who is capable of virtue in all things. As he is just in the preaching of the Risen one

[3] Peter as head: See p. 321.

[4] Forget: This verb is in the singular, the following verbs are in the plural.

[5] For the story of Juda and the cross see M.X., II, 87 and n. 6 ad loc.in Thomson's translation.

[6] Soon: *vaŀiw*, perhaps "in the morning."

and fearlessly speaks out among the crucifiers, do you also hasten, Peter. Do not hinder so many apostles whom you have brought down to the lakeshore. I do not say: "Do not say I go to fish." If that were so, go. Who knows, you understand well. Who can be teacher for you? For behold you have the grace of teaching of the holy Spirit. But it seems to me today, you still hesitate to go. For fishermen have one grace, and other arts a different one. You do not have the grace of fishermen, nor the art of sailing boats. For although you were such once, you abandoned it; and the leaving it did not come from you but from the one who chose you. If you wish, remember the saying that he spoke: "Abandon the trade of fishing, and I shall make you fishers of men"[7]. You are a catcher of mankind, consequently you cannot go fishing[8]. "And they embarked, says [scripture], on a boat; and all night they laboured but caught nothing"[9]. Rightly and truly. The night belongs to all who go around in the world without God. And their bosom is devoid of the catching of life, which only believers grasp with the help of their Lord.

"Now when it became dawn, the Lord appeared to them standing on the shore of the lake"[10]. Who has ever seen the sun appear before the light?[11] This only was seen at the lake of Tiberias. The spiritual sun descended from heaven to earth, stood on the shore of the lake, and kept enclosed in himself the rays of his incomprehensible light. Well do I say that he kept

[7] Only the second phrase occurs in Mt. 4.19; Mk. 1.17.

[8] In Armenian "fisherman" is "catcher of fish." Hence the term "catcher, hunter [*orsord*] can be used of other prey where "hunter" in English loses the verbal parallel.

[9] Jn. 21.3.

[10] Jn. 21.4.

[11] The image of Christ as sun is based on Mal. 4.2; see also below, p. 347, and the *Teaching*, 566. For this common motif see in general Lampe, s.v. *helios*.

them enclosed, because it is impossible to see that sun. He comes along the lake, as on the first occasion before he had instructed and **[p. 331]** drawn them from the lake and brought them to the rank of apostleship[12]. In the same fashion he acts also now. "Children, he says, do you have anything to eat?"[13] The eating was indeed for children. I earlier plucked you from the world, he says, and brought you to manhood, making you pass through many stages of virtue until you could receive the holy Spirit, through whom heaven and earth were completed. You once more are children, and you only think a child's [thoughts] and busy yourselves with the same. See, behold, you cannot at all fill your needs without me, hence you have nothing. For if you did have [something], I would not have asked but merely ordered [you] to bring it. For that reason I asked, because you did not have. Not that I did not know your lack, but in order that I might teach you what is right: to confess your ignorance. If you were lacking fish and you had great need at this time, for which reason you had laboured all night, why did you not throw your nets in my name, because you were familiar with my name? Often you have heard in whose name the demons obeyed you. Was it not in the name of Jesus Christ? Jesus Christ, the one from Nazareth; and Nazareth borders your land, and especially this lake. Around this same lake so many signs and miracles were performed, and many wonders, yet you still did not understand? So then, you are still in the same density of body, and you have not been unburdened of the prior heaviness? I do not mean from your sense of feeling, but from your feeble minds which did not let the divine plantings grow.

[12] Mt. 4.18; Mk. 1.16.
[13] Jn. 21.5.

"So come, he says, cast your nets[14] to the right side of your boat. For what you cast without me is night and the left-hand side; but what you cast with me is daytime and the right-hand side. If it is the right-hand, there you will find; and when you find, do not deny the grace of the knowledge of the holy Spirit, so that you may keep it firm in your souls." Having done this, they brought in a multitude of fish, and so many that they needed helpers. As they dragged in the net they exerted great effort until they had brought it to dry land. Peter was greatly astonished, **[p. 332]** not only at the multitude, but at how big they were and incalculably many; yet the net was not broken. Because they were not accustomed to find such a catch, they reckoned it a sign and not a chance catch. Therefore John said: "It is the Lord"[15]. From John's words and from the command of the Lord who said "right-hand side," Peter was aroused and cast himself naked into the lake, well before he could bring the boat to the Lord. Filled with awe and joy, he could not think aright, but turned his mind to that same previous habit, as if lacking food and rest. Therefore the Lord had pity on them, and at that spot made preparation for a meal. But none of the disciples dared ask: "Who are you?" For they knew that it was the Lord. Behold they truly knew [him], but not according to his previous likeness. Then Jesus approached even nearer, and in accordance with his earlier custom gave them a blessing, and shared with them in the food, and fulfilled and completed the revelation of the Trinity after the resurrection[16].

[14] Nets: *gorcik'*, lit. "tools," not *urkan*, the "net" in Jn. 21.6. In what follows I have translated *gorci(k')* as "net," since a literal rendering would not recall in English the traditional account of this episode.

[15] In Jn. 21.7 the disciple "whom Jesus loved" is not named.

[16] Trinity: because this was the third appearance, Jn. 21.14.

But I know what you are about to say to me: "All this the evangelist related to us. So for what purpose was the revelation of the Lord on the lake, or the multitude of fishes, and the not-splitting of the net, and the placing of the bread and fish on the coals?" May the same Jesus Christ our Lord, who in his benevolence revealed himself to his disciples, also show us the secrets of his parables[17], not only on the lake of Tiberias, but at all times and in all places — not only so that we may know and speak his commandments, but that we may also love him with all our power and not for the reason of the mediator's signs. For there are many among mankind who love God from the successes of the world; and there are also some who on being reprimanded by their deeds turn to repentance and love God. But those who are valiant and perfect in everything dedicate themselves to piety right from childhood, and not **[p. 333]** in search of signs and miracles, and are far from shameful deeds of the world. These are they who are superior to the triple number, with which there is no comparison from created things at all. But the Godhead is benevolent, receives the triple form[18], and they all move around in the divine mansions. As for us, brethren, although we are not of the first, yet let us follow the last. Let us beg the same Lord so that he may receive us too in the mercy of his love, just as he granted forgiveness to the others, and make us worthy at all times to follow the word of the holy gospel, to apply ourselves to it, to love it, to study it, and through it to reach the fulfilment of the promised tidings.

Even more must one understand this, that the sea of Tiberias is not a part of the undivided great sea, but an individual separate entity. It is called "lake" and not "sea;" and the world is the equal

[17] Parables: *aṙakk'*, which can also be used for "allegories, figures, types," in a more general sense.

[18] Form: lit. "part, *hatac.*"

to a sea and not a lake[19]. As it appears, before the coming of the Lord the terrestrial [creatures] resembled the aquatic ones without a leader or guide. In a turbulent way of life, they despoiled and destroyed each other without remorse or respect; not recognising the Creator of creation, as if at night and in dense darkeness they were totally unable to look upwards. They resembled great fish which swallow little ones indiscriminately, yet themselves are swallowed by even bigger ones[20], and they do not think at all that there are other creatures superior to us, just as the holy prophet complained: "Why did you look on the disdainful, and pay no heed when the impious swallowed the just; and you will make men like the fishes of the sea, and like the reptiles who have no leader"[21]. As is clear, this reproach concerns the patience of God. "Why, he says, did you allow it from those times?" The prophet is afflicted through the holy Spirit; he cannot see the affliction of the miserable. "Hasten, he says, come Lord, and be revealed, approach for [our] salvation; remove the world from the sea of sin[22] so that they may recognise you as Lord and Creator, ruler and leader of life; so that they not become aquatic beasts, but men earthly and heavenly, the image and form of spiritual power. **[p. 334]** For which reason "cast to the right-hand side of your boat."

Who is it who will say this? He who sits at the right-hand of the Father in heaven says to the disciples: "I shall seat you at the right-hand of the Father[23], and I shall make everything successful

[19] In this sentence Elishe uses the diminutive *covak* for the first "lake," and *lič* for the second "lake." "Sea" renders *cov*, standard in Armenian for "lake" as well as "sea."

[20] The image is reminiscent of Basil, *Hexaemeron*, VII 3, but Elishe does not use the wording of the Armenian version.

[21] Hab. 1.13.

[22] Sea of sin: as p. 328 above.

[23] Mt. 19.28-9, Lk. 22.30.

for you. There is no part of darkness in you, and no section of the left. Do not hunt at night, since the light is far from it, and many stumble through it. You are children of light, and sons of the daytime. Just as you are sons of light, likewise let your works shine in the world[24], and let the world follow you to the light of life. Do not cast your nets to the left side, because those who are sons of the left are also offspring of the power of darkness. Just as they have no part or share in success, likewise may you not have a part or share in the left-hand side.

When Peter and his companions heard this with their minds rather than with their ears[25], they cast the net on the right-hand side of the boat, and caught 153 fish. As is clear, the format of understanding is as follows — just as among the ancients some made use of rational wisdom, yet they were not found at all lacking in heavenly wisdom. Everything, they said, which is triple is divisible. Now what is divisible has thereby affinity to unity and [possesses] impassibility of abundance[26]. The number of the fishes is divisible into three fifties and one threesome, and they are linked to each other in unity. In the three fifties, in which is seen six parts by subdividing, existence derives at the beginning. But then by compounding it comes down to the same number, which we call fiftieth, which Moses legislated by calling it jubilee[27], and giving rest from the land and granting freedom from the servitude of mankind. Now in all this which Moses ordained as temporal laws, his expectation with regard to the

[24] Mt. 5.16.

[25] Since the above words are not attested as such in the gospels!

[26] Impassibility of abundance: *anaxtut'iwn harstut'ean.* The sense here of the last word, "richness, wealth, abundance," is unclear.

[27] Jubilee: But in Lev. ch. 5, this is called the "year of forgiveness, *am t'ołut'ean.*" The word *yobelean* only appears in Josh. 6.4, 6, associated with the horns.

people was fulfilled. But the truth was revealed to all races of mankind, as the number of the fishes makes clear. For the ordinance of the laws was given by the Lord. But where the Lord himself was in person, there was no further mystery but true revelation, **[p. 335]** just as we expounded very clearly in our homily. For the multitude of the three fifties was the whole world, and the days and months and years and times and living things. For it is material and begotten and [subject to] the passion of corruption, for which a passionless helper was necessary, as appears very clearly the number of the three fish mentioned simply by itself. Because they are not sixes, if they increase and complete the number of twelve, or twelves, which the number six will constitute by doubling[28]. But he said three, not more and not less. For it was the Lord's command, and it was the right-hand side and the mystery was speculation[29].

What is greater than this task, which is completed through the Word of God, and he himself appears imprinted on the operation? For the holy Trinity is indivisible, and [yet] we have seen him individualised without compactness, just as in the number of the fishes the Father was partner with the Son[30], and the holy Spirit a supportive help for the Apostles. They hunted for fish openly in the sea, and through the fish it appears that they hunted the whole world, not from water to dry land but from the arid dry-land to the water of life. For men in their need hunt fish from the sea to dry land and from life to death. And they never allow themselves to be hunted, because they are mortal both themselves and their prey. But the living God, giver and bestower of life to all

[28] This sentence I fail to comprehend at all.

[29] Speculation: *tesaworut'iwn*, with a wide range of meanings like the Greek *theoria*.

[30] Partner: *orsakic'*, as in Lk. 5.7, i.e. "partner in hunting;" see p. 330.

dead [natures][31], hunts prey from death to life, and to a life not insignificant but timeless and which does not pass away. Not only does he hunt, but he himself is hunted by the prey, not supposedly but in truth. For he is fearless and without hesitation, unseparated and indivisible. Just as he linked himself to the number of the fish in threefold form without envy of malevolence, in the same manner he was hunted by his own prey; and he gave himself as bait[32] for food, so that at the same time he might be sea and place and hook and food and fisherman. And very rightly so. For unfailing and inexhaustible food is life. Everyone who eats of life **[p. 336]** thereby gains life, and life does not die but even more multiplies and increases and rejoices and is happy.

Although I spoke in abbreviated fashion, I shall give an example of the truth, which has similarity but not indeed the essence. But I shall speak not my own [words] but those of the same Word of life. For when the tempter came up to him, he said to him, tempting: "If you are really the Son of God, tell these stones to become bread"[33]. Then he heard as response not only "living by bread" but "by the word of God." The word of God is the Son of God, and he gives himself as food, yet is not at all ashamed. As he nourishes this world without effort, so he is eaten [for][34] the world without being cut up or divided. But I question that same tempter: "What do you eat? You have no land; you have no livelihood or harvest. It is clear that you do not live by bread, nor by any other solid food. Behold, it appeared that you are nourished by the word of God. For although you are not worthy, yet God is

[31] Dead: *meřelut'iwnk'*, pl. of the abstract noun.

[32] Bait: *xani*, see Aa 81 for this theme, which is common in Armenian.

[33] Mt. 4.3.

[34] The sense is unclear, there being no preposition with "world," which is in the genitive/dative case.

beneficent; and he himself remains without being consumed or loss. This is what I meant by: "He hunts mortals for life, and himself is hunted; and by making himself equal with corruptible prey, both secretly and openly he extricates [them] from corruption."

"And all the fishes were very large"[35]. Why are you astonished at that? When God hunts fish, nothing is hidden from his all-seeing eye. When he wishes, the largest ones; when he wishes, the small ones; and when he wishes, the medium ones. With these parts three in number, they are all his. It is thus with the fishes. First he hunted the largest ones, because it was a mystery and not the truth. But for the selection of the Apostles it was not thus: first the small, and then the large. I said small, and rightly. Not only are they small, but also ignorant and Galileans, uncouth in speech, provincial in origin, poor and needy. What is poorer than fishermen, or more foolish than the same? For all his worries are for the water-going skiff, and his speech is with the irrational fish. It appears that they are not only the most ignorant of men, **[p. 337]** but also the most rustic. I bear you witness that they are not merely as humble as we said, but many times more than that. But do not pay attention to such poverty, which is not of their own will but from the misfortunes of the world. For men attain lordly power by motives of avarice. They despoil and deprive their fellows, and bring them to great misery.

Look at the benevolence of God and see why the coming of the Lord to this world occurred. Was it not so that he might prevent all this and effect equality of life? So whom did you have chosen, you who abhor the poor and flee from the needy, since: "By the wisdom of God the world did not recognise God?"[36] It

[35] Very large: *mecamec* as Jn. 21.11.

[36] I Cor. 1.21.

was necessary to choose the foolish. Furthermore, those who were powerful not only were impious against God, but also inflicted great oppression on the very weak. Therefore God chose the weak of this world, so that he might put the strong to shame[37]. Just as through the weak he shamed the strong, likewise through the foolish he will silence the wise. "For God chose, he says;" and where there is God's choice, there is no weakness or foolishness. Just as he brought this world into existence from non-existence, likewise from weakness he brought it to strength, and from poverty to riches. For he makes the world new. I do not mean the matter or the form; but the former [people] who had been willingly corrupted he brought back anew to the same [original] nature. First those through whom he renews[38] them he made new and wealthy, at the same time also wise. Of their wisdom [he is] the leader and teacher; and with them the holy Spirit is co-worker, through whom everything had been created previously.

Do you see that thereafter they do not go around the lake in Galilee, but around the great sea; and the "sea," not water, but islands and all the dry land. And they possessed not the customary net, but a new one wherewith they themselves were hunted, which does not tear. For the net is long, but longer than the net is the line of the net. For they put the bait **[p. 338]** in the middle and they spread the net over the whole earth.

They are twelve in number. The lines of the net are two, and four the ends of the lines, and three by three take up each end, because double three is perfect firmness. One side to the west, the equal to it on the east, and two to the north and south. The

[37] I Cor. 1.27.

[38] Renews: The printed text has *norogen*, in the plural. I suggest *norogēn*, 3p.s. with the obligatory suffix *n* after the preceding relative pronoun.

round circle[39] enclosed the whole world. They do not pull the net in each one's direction, but they are all in unison. Where the bait has been put, to there they gather all [the fish] — for life and not death, because it is living food, for the living and not for the dead.

But I know what you are going to say. What advantage is it, you say? He drew from the lake, and in the sea again hunted fish. I did not say that, brother. But because you are in search of wisdom, do you yourself learn the parable of the net which the Lord previously adumbrated[40]. Furthermore you love the powerful. Whoever among mankind was stronger than this one, who can embrace the whole world in a single unity? No one will appear richer than they. If your mind will happily agree to these three parts, I shall explain to you both the net and the netsmen, and I shall not hide from you the catch of the fishes. But because of the multitude, if you can, count them. I cannot. The sea is this world, the net the preaching of the Lord, the points of the net the four gospels, the holders of the net the twelve apostles, the catch of the fishes all the nations of the gentiles, while the fish-hook in the middle is the body and blood of our Lord Jesus Christ. The centre of all is the true faith. For the Godhead is elevated; but the nature of mankind occupies the lower region of the earth. The power of the Spirit was humbled from above to below, and faith was set upright from below to above. Grasping the power [of the Spirit], [faith] stands secured by those below, so that it may pull them up.

Now since we came up from the sea to the dry land[41], and from the fish we attained the race of mankind, come and see the twelve.

[39] Round circle: *bolorak parurajew*. This spoils the image of the four-cornered net! Cf. the four sides of the world on p. 328.

[40] Adumbrated: *nmanec'oyc'*, lit. "made a likeness."

[41] See p. 333 for the sinful aquatic creatures.

[**p. 339**] Not only are the net-holders in the sea, but [they are] also sailors. On the dry land [they are] messengers, and in the war soldiers, and in the world citizens; and they are also legislators. Consequently no more do they need any of mankind for assistance; because the one who gives strength to all is with them, they are fearless and unhesitating. Whence they fled, stricken with fear — from Jerusalem — thence they made the beginning of their new preaching. Boldly they teach, not in some secret and hidden corner, but inside the very temple where all the world was gathered. Incessantly adducing the name of Jesus, they demonstrate many signs and miracles in front of all. Not suddenly do they depart from the desirable city; nor do they reckon the place unworthy, where the Lord of all died unworthily, but as a great boast and the life of all creatures. With their voice they speak out, with their hand they point, with their eye they see Bethlehem, where he was born; Nazareth, where he grew up; Galilee, where he lived; Golgotha, where he was crucified; the tomb, whence he arose; the Mount of Olives, whence he ascended; heaven, where he sat down at the right hand of the Father.

Who then could be richer than the Apostles, or wiser than those who know all this? He is also a more liberal giver. The weak [man] who sat at the beautiful gate of the temple received individually the mites, and scarcely filled his daily fare[42]. See the wealth of the apostles, and therewith their liberality. Not only did they give the rations of a day and of a month, but for all the days of his life. For he received healing; not only was he cured of temporal pains, but through his faith he also inherited eternal life.

So where the Lord began to reveal his divinity to the world, there the apostles too made a beginning. Often they taught them

[42] Cf. Acts. 3.2.

and bore witness to the priests and interpreters[43] that: "I have no other name under heaven whereby healing is effected, save only the name of our Lord Jesus Christ[44]. For Jesus and Christ, **[p. 340]** because of his love for mankind, incarnated himself[45] into bodily form so that bodily [creatures] might be able to see him and learn — both that through him heaven and earth were made, and that he is the legislator through Moses. Concerning him the prophets preached in former times; and the day of his coming our patriarchs and kings desired to see"[46]. With all this testimony the apostles spoke with the whole multitude, until they persuaded even the high-priest Caiaphas to listen to him through them.

They were so bold that saint Stephen, although he was younger than the others in age, for the love which he had for Christ hastened to shed his own blood for his sake, so that his testimony might be not only through words but also with great power, even to death. See the power of the crucified one, to what heights he drew the world, as he previously said: "When I am raised up, I shall draw all to me"[47]. For this same Stephen, while he was still of sound body, knew only speaking in the name of Jesus Christ. For although he possessed grace and performed great signs, yet he had not seen him face to face. So that day stones showered down on him, blood flowed over his face, his body fell to the ground. To that he paid no attention; looking upwards he opened heaven[48], he saw Christ at the right hand of the Father, and he prayed for

[43] Interpreters: as p. 247 above. In Acts 4.1 the text has "Sadducees."

[44] Acts. 4.12.

[45] Incarnated himself: *t'anjrac'oyc' zink'n*. For *t'anjr*, "dense, heavy," in the sense of "body" see p. 256 above and the Introduction. With reference to the Incarnation cf. Lampe, s.v. *pachuno*.

[46] Cf. Mat. 13.17, Jn. 8.56.

[47] Jn. 12.32.

[48] Sic! Cf. Acts 7.55.

his slayers. This was an imitation of Christ's death, and prayer for his prayers. For just as he [prayed] for his crucifiers, so did he pray for those stoning him.

But perhaps someone may say: "What advantage would there be to pray for the evil ones that they may increase even more in wickedness?" It is not so. Do not think this at all. See the power of prayer and rejoice at the fruit which it produced. Indeed it was Saul who had him stoned, and Stephen who prayed: "Father, forgive them because they do not know that they do"[49]. Truly did he pray, and justly he heard him. For not only did he forgive them their sins, but he joined them to the rank of the apostles.

[p. 341] So they fulfilled all his testimony by words and deeds in Jerusalem in front of the high priests. And they left there James in place of them all, reckoning that man's nobility sufficient, so that they would not leave empty the place from which the Lord had commanded them not to depart[50]. They themselves took by lot all races and peoples, and hastened to the preaching of the gospel. Did you see at that time they were so slothful that the Lord himself could scarcely wake them from sleep?[51] But today, ceaselessly day and night they are urgently zealous to speak and to hear and to carry out all the wishes of their Creator — and especially when they saw the raging wolf, who was mingling with and slaughtering all the shepherdless flock. As that same great James said to Peter: "Hasten to Caesarea Stratoneanc'[52]. For there

[49] Acts 7.60.

[50] Acts 1.4.

[51] Cf. p. 254 above.

[52] *Kesaria Stratoneanc'*. I.e. Caesarea Stratonis, on the coast, to be distinguished from Caesarea Philippi. *Stratoneanc'* does not appear in the Armenian bible or apocryphal Acts.

is Simon the magician[53], who has clothed himself with demons like a garment, and against souls has Satan as weapon. For not he alone has gone astray onto the path of destruction, but also all those who heed him. So hurry, brother, arrive quickly to help the multitude who are perishing through ignorance, because you will find for yourself many helpers there." Having said this, James entrusted him to the holy Spirit and sent him on his way, while he himself remained there.

When Peter arrived at the populous city by the grace of our Lord Jesus Christ, through great signs and wonders he confirmed many of the people. He admonished backsliding, expelled the wicked beast, rescued the innocent flock from error, and by the grace of the holy Spirit even expelled death from their borders. While he was in Caesarea Stratoneanc', a certain woman by the name of Aycemnik was a disciple of the apostles, and was overseer of the orphans and widows in the city of Lydda[54]. It happened at that same time that she died, and when Peter arrived he restored the departed one [to life] to the astonishment of the inhabitants of the land. And many myriads were added to the number of the believers. When James heard this about Peter, he rejoiced and was glad in the holy Spirit. And even more boldly he bore testimony **[p. 342]** to the name of the Lord in front of all the people, and remained firm in the same.

Now Peter healed the wounds of those who had been afflicted by the evil poisonous beast, and he taught them all to turn from the erroneous worship of idols to the one God Father of all, who

[53] According to Acts, ch.8, Simon was in Samaria. But Elishe is following the story in the apocryphal *Acts of Peter and Paul*, where Caesarea is named. See *Ankanon Girk'*, III, p. 15.

[54] *Aycemnik* is Armenian for "gazelle," the Dorcas of Acts 9.36. But there she is said to be at Joppa [though "Lydda was nigh to Joppa," v.38].

created everything, and to the Only-begotten who came in his own benevolence and revealed himself to the race of mankind, so that not only by listening might they know God, but also by looking and seeing and speaking with him in close proximity they might recognise [him] and be recognised. As indeed happened. For while Peter was in the city of Joppa, an angel of the Lord appeared to Cornelius in Caesarea, who was of the race of Gentiles and through his works was superior to all the Israelites, save only that he lacked knowledge of Jesus Christ and the reception of baptism in his name. He immediately commanded Peter to be summoned to his house[55].

See the works of the large net which was not torn and holds the great fishes. For just as the holy Spirit was revealed to Peter in the likeness of a linen container held up at the four corners[56], it contained all living creatures, clean and unclean, small and large, not only from water but also from dry land. If you remember, I said earlier that there were four corners of the heavenly net, and it contained within it the four corners of this world[57]. So when you hear of the descent of the container from heaven to earth, do not imagine in your mind a cord to the linen container, or some material element, because no single part of created things can hold in itself all creatures. But understand there the power of the holy Spirit through whom everything was created. He extended himself into the likeness of a linen container. Why indeed? Because a container of linen is purest and has a shining appearance. It gathered all the races which were clean and those who were not clean — according to the visible appearance as if it descended from heaven to

[55] Acts 10.5.

[56] Acts 10.11. Elishe clearly states that the Spirit was revealed, rather than that the Spirit revealed the net.

[57] For the elaborate simile of the net see p. 338 above.

earth. But according to the spiritual interpretation[58] **[p. 343]** it brought earthly [creatures] close to heavenly ones. To Peter clearly [were revealed] the living creatures which were given for the food of mankind; and everything was there which the law commanded to eat and what it forbad. Because Peter was hungry, food appeared to him in a great vision, teaching him at the same time the perfect knowledge of God. "If you are hungry for food, said [the voice], kill and eat"[59]. But he had recourse to the custom of the law. "I have not eaten anything common or unclean." Then he heard the response: "What God purifies, do you not reckon foul"[60]. So how did he purify them? For on the linen he saw all creatures. And if the linen container is the likeness of the creative Spirit, and the creatures in it are the nations of the Gentiles, then they were purified in that same [container] on which they were placed. For everyone who approaches the holy Spirit with true faith is thereby rendered spiritual[61], because he makes the same answer: "What God has purified." The vision was divine and human. So if God purified and you are hungry for food, then God is hungry for the portion of righteousness.

So who is holy according to your wishes? Perhaps you will say: the sons of the law. They are not only not pure, but became very befouled. I know that you abhor the Gentiles and do not wish to approach them, because they are uncircumcised in body but not in heart. For this I do not blame [you]. But arise and go to the house of the Gentiles, and teach them not to be circumcised but to be baptised. There you will see a great revelation of the holy

[58] For the contrast between visible things and spiritual interpretations see p. 328 above.

[59] Only the last three words appear in Acts 10.13.

[60] Acts 10.14-15.

[61] Rendered spiritual: *hogiac'aw*, lit. "became spirit."

Spirit. What is greater than the appearance of an angel to a man, as happened to Cornelius? Not only was he seen by him, but he also gave him much praise. "Your prayers, he said, have been heard, and your supplications went up before God"[62]. So what further did this man need? By his prayers he was pure, by giving gifts benevolent. Himself a believer, he kept his family according to the will of righteousness. In his great authority he was able to be a leader of others to good works.

So see the power of Christ, because not a single **[p. 344]** word was false of the sayings of the Lord: "For John baptised in water, but you shall be baptised in the holy Spirit"[63]. The holy Spirit himself came to Cornelius, yet was unable to ordain[64] the man for baptism. Peter came, and on his entrance into the centurion's palace all those in the house were filled with the holy Spirit and spoke amazing tongues. When Peter realised this, he immediately baptised them all.

What need was there for those filled with the Spirit to be baptised in water, I shall ask you? For it would be right to baptise not only men who have received the Spirit, but also the holy Spirit; as indeed happened. For those who had received the holy Spirit were also ordained by Peter for the baptism of the font. So then the Spirit was baptised with them. Now if the holy Spirit will not be baptised with the [persons] baptised, the baptism is not called complete, but a washing of water. Just as some were baptised with water without receiving the holy Spirit, then the apostles made [them] worthy of a second baptism so that they might receive the holy Spirit. For the origin of baptism was God's and not man's.

62 Acts 10.4.

63 Acts 1.5.

64 Ordain: *jeṙnadrel*, "place one's hand on," not used in this connection in Acts.

God received baptism from a man, since when the Lord spoke to John he said: "Permit now that we fulfil all righteousness"[65]. The fulfilment of righteousness is to know truly the holy Trinity, and this knowledge was revealed to us at the baptism of the Son[66]. The Father bore witness through a voice, and the holy Spirit appeared visibly, and the Son was baptised truly, and righteousness was fulfilled without lack. Likewise in the house of Cornelius the Father was revealed through the angel, the holy Spirit filled them all, Peter baptised everyone in the name of Jesus Christ. This the Lord previously declared: "The kingdom of heaven is like a net thrown into the sea. It brings and gathers from all nations, from which they take up the useful and throw out the useless"[67]. Thus it is with regard to the nets of men; but for the heavenly one not so. There is no useless and vile there; but all are select, and there is no base one among them. Likewise [they are] very large[68]. But if someone willingly **[p. 345]** becomes worthless and wicked and goes out of the spiritual net, then he is not only thrown out but also trampled by those who are even more wicked than himself.

[65] Mt. 3.15.

[66] The Trinity was revealed at Christ's baptism; cf. Elishe, *On Baptism*, p. 212.

[67] Mt. 13.47.

[68] As of the fishes caught in the lake of Tiberias.

[*On the Preaching of the Apostles*][1]

[p. 345] Now the origin of the baptism of the Son was in the Jordan river. It is spread abroad in Judaea, increases and reaches the shore of the great sea; from [that] origin it becomes once more a beginning in the house of the centurion, then it is scattered and spread through all nations of the Gentiles. For when Peter saw that even to the Gentiles was given the grace of the holy Spirit, he himself went up to Jerusalem and showed [what had happened] to James[2]. Although those of the circumcision had scruples about him, yet when they heard from Peter reliable testimony concerning the power of the holy Spirit — that very openly he had appeared also among the Gentiles as in our midst — thenceforth they had no scruples about Peter, but they all made haste to each one's region according to the guidance of the holy Spirit. Peter himself [went] to the great Rome; Mark to Alexandria; Thomas to the land of the Indians, as also Thaddaeus set out for the east; Philip instructed the eunuch on the chariot and baptised him, and sent him by the power of the holy Spirit to Ethiopia[3]; John was in Asia[4], like Andrew in the regions of the north. They all

[1] There is no title in the text, but the editors so mark this section in the headers.

[2] Acts 11.4, but James is not mentioned there.

[3] Acts 8.27-39.

[4] Rev. 1.4.

made haste: some to distant islands, others to nooks and crannies on dry land; they spread out into all regions of the earth[5]. Paul made a beginning of baptising in Damascus[6], and in ceaseless journeys went from Jerusalem as far as Illyricum[7].

These are great works and a wonderful sight. For they did not preach in some corner, nor did they proclaim the name of Jesus Christ in secret but openly, with a loud voice, in great cities where princes resided. Even in great Rome, where the capital was; and in Athens, where there were the most erudite of the philosophers and the legislators of [various] lands; and in Ephesus, where there were famous temples and open **[p. 346]** cults of the heathen religion; and in barbarous islands, whose [inhabitants] were nothing less than savage beasts in their natural habits; and in the land of the Egyptians, who were particularly enmeshed in magic; and [where] demons in solid form[8] went around among the population, and the Persian religion [was observed], and they gave themselves over indiscriminately to immoral prostitution. Furthermore, who could describe all the evils which were practised among the heathen?[9] For not only did they sacrifice living animals to the demons, but they also sacrificed their own sons and daughters, dedicating them for slaughter and bringing them to be burned, and were indiscriminate to all evil deeds. Some in barbarous islands even had adopted without scruple or shame the custom of sacrificing and eating their own fellows — not merely strangers

[5] Elishe uses the Apocryphal Acts in addition to the NT.

[6] Acts 9.18.

[7] Rom. 15.19.

[8] In solid form: *t'anjrac'ealk'*. For *t'anjr*, "solid, dense," in the context of human form and Incarnation see p. 256 above.

[9] Heathen: The Armenian *het'anos* is ambiguous, rendering the Greek *ethne*, "Gentiles," as well as "heathen" in the modern sense.

who came among them, but even relatives from their own clan, as the *History of Andrew* very clearly indicates to us, who was saved by the evangelist Matthew[10].

So why should I describe them individually? As we said above, in accordance with the complaint of the prophet, men had become like wild animals, and like reptiles on dry land and like fish of the sea. They slew each other and were slain by each other. But on the coming of our Lord Jesus Christ, through the twelve apostles whom he had previously chosen, he saved and rescued all nations of men. The preaching was short on words, but the deeds were very great and most powerful. For not only did they reprove the heathen in many words, and according to the details of their accumulated sins expound their admonitions, but [they spoke] as follows: "Abstain from fornication and the blood of sacrifices, and from eating things strangled"[11]. Observing this, they were to receive baptism in the name of our Lord Jesus Christ, and through him to recognize the holy Spirit and the Father of all. The apostles reckoned this short message sufficient for the total fulfilment of righteousness. For although the heathens had gone raving after the error of demons and unworthy fornication, yet they had laws of civilization[12] **[p. 347]** which debarred theft and rapine and indiscriminate killing. Men reckoned the set laws as sufficient for control of the body.

Now because of the outpouring of the Spirit, to which princes and kings paid no heed, through these three canonical sayings,

10 See "Concerning Andrew the apostle and his miracles which the Lord worked through him and Matthew in the Land of the Cannibals," *Ankanon Girk'*, III, 124-145.

11 Acts 15.29.

12 Laws of civilization: cf. the "natural law," as discussed by Mxit'ar Goš, *Datastanagirk'*, p. 23.

with the great power of signs and miracles in all aspects of righteousness which God accomplished through the apostles, he cast awe and fear on all the idolators. For the demons were expelled, sacrifices stopped, the smoke of offerings ceased, the songs of lewdness were silenced, the error of magic terminated, fornication was put to shame, marriage made chaste, holiness disclosed.

All this occurred at the dawn of the spiritual sun among the heathen[13]. When the darkness of error had been dissipated and stripped from them, then they were able to see the light of the grace of the holy Spirit, to which was opposed the first-born of Satan, Simon, who deceived and led astray many myriads and called himself a heavenly power who had come for the salvation of the race of mankind[14]. When Peter arrived, by the power of the Spirit not only did he admonish and chastise him, but he withdrew a multitude of men from him and confirmed them in the truth of the preaching of the gospel. Then [Simon] was expelled from the land; he took to the sea and crossed over to Rome. Peter followed, but not in haste; rather he passed by the cities of Phoenicia, made signs and miracles in the name of Jesus Christ, and established many congregations. He followed the magician and reached Rome. He did not again expell him from the city, but reprimanded him with words, and with signs confirmed the city. Simon, seized by the demons, raised himself a little above the city, and there in front of all fell down and was dashed to pieces. They were not only eye-witnesses, but with their own hands they dragged [the body] and cast it out of the city. On seeing this a multitude of men and women affirmed the truth of the preaching

[13] Spiritual sun: Mal. 4.2; see p. 330.

[14] Acts 8.9. But Elishe is following the "Acts of Peter and Paul," *Ankanon Girk'*, III 1-45.

of the gospel. **[p. 348]** They were baptised by Peter and became many congregations. It was reported even to the royal palace, and they firmly accepted the gospel. Made worthy of the grace of martyrdom, they were put to death.

Then Peter also, the chief of the apostles, in that same city received sentence of death in the likeness of Christ's cross[15]. He placed a firm rock as foundation of the church and fulfilled the word of the Lord, who said: "You are a rock, and on this rock I shall build my church"[16]. He was indeed a rock of the true tradition of the faith. Just as Peter built himself for Christ through the testimony of death, so was the church built on Peter's faith, not only in Rome but also throughout all cities and villages, from the greatest to the smallest: the same faith, the same foundation, and the same establishment. For one is the Lord, and one baptism[17], whereby we have received forgiveness of sins and life for our souls in the name of our Lord Jesus Christ.

Just as Peter established the church in Rome, likewise the other apostles according to each one's allotted lands, where they had been ordered to fulfil the gospel of Christ. God gave them grace by the holy Spirit, and through them carried out signs and great miracles. They cured diseases of the body and healed illnesses of the soul; they even raised the dead. They appeared more glorious than the nature of mankind among the heathen, who took bulls and crowns and offered sacrifices as if to God[18]. They were so distinguished by heavenly revelations and given such wisdom by the holy Spirit that they brought the most erudite of the philosophers

[15] The "Acts of Peter and Paul" end with the crucifixion of Peter and the beheading of Paul.

[16] Mt. 16.18.

[17] Eph. 4.5.

[18] Acts 14.12.

into agreement, confirmed him in the true faith, and made him a co-worker of the gospel[19].

This was a new and wonderful vision. The Galileans became Romans; and those who were the weakest of all fought with strength not only against princes and prefects[20], but against emperors and their armies. [**p. 349**] Those who had been raised without education by the lake of Gennesaret disputed with Athenians. Not only did they prevail and silence them, but they removed them from their original knowledge and taught and confirmed them in the grace of the holy Spirit.

Who indeed could express their greatness? They themselves were homeless and without a city on earth, yet to others they promised mansions and cities in heaven. They themselves were poor; and the riches of others they plundered. They were persecuted by men, yet expelled demons from the world. Their bodies were covered with beatings, yet they cured the wounds of others from irremediable afflictions. They were hungry for bread, yet fed spiritual food to many. They were thirsty for water, but proffered to all the cup of salvation. They were imprisoned, yet they broke the bonds of sin of others. They were condemned and released the condemned. They were condemned to death, yet made forgiveness for mortals. They appeared on earth, and moved around in heaven. They struggled with men, and conquered demons. They received whippings on their own bodies, and the hosts of demons were tormented.

I cannot find on earth a comparison for the twelve apostles. For they were more glorious than the flowering plains, and taller than the highest mountains. They were greater than the vastness of the

[19] I.e. Dionysius the Areopagite; Acts, ch. 17.

[20] Prefects: *k'ałak'apet*, as Acts 17.6, 8.

sea, and more profound than its depths. They took their leave from this earth, and became higher than heaven. So to whom shall I liken them, and whom shall I adduce as parallel? If I call them clouds, they are not comparable. Clouds receive water from the sea and scatter it over the earth. But these have the holy Spirit with them, not only by raining and scattering, but they immerse totally and bury in the waters of the font, and make heavenly plants, a living plant which passes not away. If I call them the moon, the moon waxes and wanes. But the apostles wax and fill without waning, and they themselves remain without passing away. And if I call them stars, the latter possess not a single glory and appear not with a single splendour, but one is large and another less, one is the morning-star, another the evening-star. But the apostles are all morning-stars, [**p. 350**] they all are glorious, they all are equally vigilant[21], united and concordant. Furthermore, what similarity have the stars and the apostles? Of the stars one is high, one is low, one is in between. The apostles are all upward-bearing and elevated. The stars only appear at night, and in the daytime are swallowed up and hidden by the light of the sun. But the apostles shine by day and by night: by day they are light for souls, and at night sobriety for souls and bodies.

The apostles are more glorious than the sun through the power of the holy Spirit. The sun has authority over the daytime; the apostles have authority over day and night. The sun is for seeing the earth and the undertaking of bodily needs. The apostles are for seeing heaven and earth, and for the understanding of souls and bodies. The sun changes and alters, but the apostles are without change or alteration, without movement. The sun rises and sets in time; the apostles announced to the world the time of the dawning of the

[21] Vigilant: *zuart'un*. For this as a name for angels see p. 278 above.

light. The sun never begets another sun; but the offspring of the apostles completed the works of their fathers. The offspring of the sun are the rays of its light, and they never enabled a blind man to receive sight. The offspring of the apostles in the holy church often gave sight to the blind, healed the lame, cast out diseases, raised the dead. The light of the sun dances around bodies, indicates visible things, and guides travellers on their journeys. The light of the preaching of the apostles also dances around bodies, and it opens the eyes of souls and leads to the heavenly city. In the light of the sun men and animals move around during the daytime, and at night they rest from their labour. In the light of the faith of the apostles heavenly and earthly ones were invited to the renewal of life, which does not pass away or diminish.

These are the apostles, who were magnified and raised up and made superior to heaven, and who reached the Father of all. They urged on the whole world to the preaching of the gospel of truth, **[p. 351]** that all might attain that same supernal city where the twelve will receive the ineffable crown of the kingdom.

As our Lord Jesus Christ three times asked the chief of the disciples: "Simon, son of Jonah, do you love me?"[22] he truthfully gave witness that he alone is worthy of perfect love, because he is Creator. He came to renew his own creatures, not through an angel and not through a prophet, and not through any other visible means, but through his own creation. For just as he created man out of his own love, likewise for love he came to seek the one who was lost. Out of his love he found the lost sheep; out of his love he raised it on to his shoulders; out of his love he caressed it and placed it in his arms; out of his love he brought and joined it to the rational flock, which grazes on spiritual pastures and rests

[22] Jn. 21.15-17. Simon: *Smawon*; for this Syriac form see Lyonnet, p. 88.

in the sheep-folds of immortality. For love Peter responded and said: "Lord, you know everything, and you are familiar with everything. If someone loves you, you know that well, I know that you question in order to test. If you ask often, you will hear the same from me. You, like God and the Son of the benevolent, loved the world without measure, and you laid yourself down for it. I, like a man, in accordance with my weakness love you. I cannot give anything, because I am poor. And if I give, it is from you that I shall take and give to you."

But who allowed you to know the reasons, or what you lack, and what will you wish to seek, and what shall I possess which I may give you? For previously you never asked me such questions. So if the question is new, I know that you are giving me some new command. Say it, my Lord, openly. I know that you do not command me what I cannot do; nor do you seek from me what I do not possess to give you.

When the Lord saw that he loved him with all his heart, and willed with all his will, and was emboldened with all his strength, because he gave his whole self to him, he entrusted to him the beginning and middle and end, childhood, youth, and old age. **[p. 352]** Into these three divisions is the visible world [divided] and the total creation comprehended. But the first is best, and the middle one inferior[23]. For when the Lord said to Peter: "Feed my lambs,"[24] he entrusted to him the innocent. And the second [command] referring to the sheep he spoke inseparably [from the first], but [its meaning] is not clear like that of "lambs." For lambs are the offspring of sheep[25], and prudent sheep [*awdi*] appear as a

[23] Inferior: *krtseragoyn*, of status, or "younger" in age.

[24] Jn. 21.15.

[25] This obscure passage depends on the distinction between various words for sheep. In Jn. 21.16-17 [the biblical text and Elishe's quotation] the usual word,

model of the right-hand side. But saying "sheep [*oč'xar*]" is a custom of men, "of the sheep" the same as "of the goat," but not very clearly and mixed, because the black one and the white one were distinguished[26], and the naturally separate were not mingled with each other. Just as the best appeared on the right-hand side, likewise the worst selected the left-hand side, by choice and not by nature.

Why should this be so? The saying is true for me from veracious natural words. The male ram[27] bears the likeness of a breath of air, yet it is a true model of the heavenly [things]. But the he-goat of the goats resembles the watery part, solidity in bodily form[28] which has the condition of corruption, and is divided and separated from rational nature, where it is seen on the left-hand side. When the Lord again said: "Pasture my cattle,"[29] this is a further great multitude and clear division. We call cattle beasts. With your single word you have enclosed and enveloped them all — the innocent and the sinners, the holy and the unholy, the necessary and the useless. Whichever are domesticated and subject to the authority of man, we call them all cattle, because they need the leadership of a shepherd[30]. Now because the flock is one and the

oč'xar is used — hence its use "as a custom of men." But here Elishe has *awdi*, which is only used in the NT in Mt. 25.32-33, with reference to the distinction between sheep and goats, the right-hand side and the left-hand. The use of different words for "sheep" clearly points to Elishe's use, or knowledge, of the Syriac. For the Greek of Jn. 21.16-17 uses *probata* in both cases, but the Syriac distinguishes *'erba* and *neqya*.

[26] Here Elishe interpolates into the NT a reference to the famous vision of St. Gregory, who saw black goats turn into white sheep, Aa 740.

[27] Male ram: *xoyn aruac'*. The following sentences are also unclear.

[28] Solidity in bodily form: *marmnajew t'anjrut'iwn*; for *t'anjr* in the context of bodies see p. 256 above.

[29] Here Elishe uses yet another word, *xašn*, which means "cattle" rather than "sheep," and is used in the Gospels only at Jn. 4.12, referring to Jacob's "cattle."

[30] Shepherd: the customary term, *hoviw*.

shepherd is one, and one are the pastures and one the sheepfold of repose for them all, the lambs and sheep and the whole multitude which he called cattle are there, especially those same apostles whom he entrusted to Peter and who shared in their preaching — all these are holy and divine lambs.

But those who by pretence were disciples of the gospel and showed to many newly formed paths were opponents of the truth. Because they had the name **[p. 353]** of Christ and demonstrated in themselves the forms of the apostles, but in their works of evil resembled Satan, they are the goats which stand on the left-hand side of their father Satan, whom they chose of their own will and with whom they shall go to their future abode. Those whom he called cattle are those who opposed the truth. They not only were an impediment and obstacle to the gospel, but they also laid hands on the holy apostles and their disciples, often beating and torturing them. Many of them they killed by the sword, like Nero and many other companions of his. Even up to today this has been done and is being done[31].

So pasture, he said, the innocent and the sinners and those who will bring death upon you. Pasture, he says, do not hesitate, just as I myself came for the salvation of all in common, of the evil and the good, and for a life of renewal, so that they might become one flock under the control of a single shepherd, they might hear the voice of the same, follow him, and receive the same life; so that they might all be innocent sheep and not ones who strike and buffet and break. So if there is anyone who will rebel against the crook of your pastoral staff and oppose the truth of this gospel, do not hesitate but take courage and strength, wage war until the death, whereby you will make me glorious.

[31] Given the history of Armenia, this reference to martyrdoms "today" is of no help in dating Elishe's Homily.

But perhaps we all desire to hear where the Lord may command the cattle to pasture, or what the pastures are, or what sort of waters they may be, or what the place of rest. Truly this is pleasant to me and to all who love to hear. For it is the [mark] of shepherd-hood to hide the life and faith of Peter. Now the cattle are the whole nation of the Gentiles. The sites of the pastures are the holy and apostolic church. The fodder is the law and prophets and apostles. The waters are the eternal news of the gospel. And where they rest at ease without fear is the supernal Jerusalem, which is the mother of us all. For there there are no goats of the left-hand side, nor butting he-goats, nor tossing rams, nor **[p. 354]** murderous bulls; nor is there anything at all harmful. But all are sincere, innocent, holy, simple, honest; not only clothed white in colour but also in soul, formed like rays, similar to the band of heavenly angels. For with them they will have a concordance of unity of voices and forms and colours. With them also they will be companions in joy, bearing crowns and approaching close to their fellow-champion, Christ[32]. To him they paid heed, of him were they disciples, him they obeyed, for him they carried out all the commandments according to his wishes. They shared the torments of his death, with him they will receive the joy that passes not away; and with him they will see the Father of all by the power of the holy Spirit, through whom they completed their earthly heroic acts. With him they will come to his second coming to judge the living and the dead and to requite each one according to their deeds, dividing each on two sides, whichever they have chosen here, some for merciless torments, others for ineffable eternal life.

[32] Champion: *nahatak*, not used of Christ in the Armenian NT. It renders the Greek *athletes*, used of Christ [see Lampe, s.v.] and of martyrs.

So sons and brothers, fathers and lords, all great ones, offspring of the baptism of the holy church, readers of the law and prophets, disciples of the news of the gospel, [let us be][33] firm in the faith of the apostles, built on the rock of establishment, looking to the heavenly hope at the coming of our Lord Jesus Christ and his meeting us all, so that we be [ready] without shame or reserve to recognise him through the signs of the nails of his passion and by the words of the written gospel. Furthermore, from our deeds we shall be known to him, so that our paths may be in accordance with the holy preaching of the apostles that "the man of God should be perfect in all truth,"[34] [and] so that we may hear the voice of the benevolent one who says to all those who keep the commandments: "Come blessed of my Father, inherit the kingdom prepared for you from the beginning of the world"[35]. With whom, to the Father and the holy Spirit, [be] glory and honour, now and always, and for ever and ever. Amen.

[33] There is no main verb for this sentence.
[34] II Tim. 3.17.
[35] Mt. 25.34.

INDEX OF SCRIPTURAL QUOTATIONS AND ALLUSIONS

GENERAL INDEX OF NAMES

PRINTED ON PERMANENT PAPER • IMPRIME SUR PAPIER PERMANENT • GEDRUKT OP DUURZAAM PAPIER - ISO 9706

ORIENTALISTE, KLEIN DALENSTRAAT 42, B-3020 HERENT